Practical
WEIGHT
TRAINING

WORKOUTS, WEIGHTS AND EQUIPMENT

Practical WEIGHT TRAINING

WORKOUTS, WEIGHTS AND EQUIPMENT

Kevin Pressley

mustard

This is a Mustard Book
Mustard is an imprint of Parragon

© Parragon 1999

Parragon
Queen Street
4 Queen Street
Bath BA1 1HE United Kingdom

First published by Parragon 1995

Designed and produced by
Touchstone, Old Chapel Studio, Plain Road,
Marden, Tonbridge, Kent TN12 9LS England
Photography by Roger Hart
Edited by Sheila James

ISBN 1-84164-131-6

Printed in Italy

Disclaimer
The exercises and advice detailed in this book assumes that you are a
normally healthy adult. Therefore the author, publishers, their servants or
agents cannot accept responsibility for loss or damage suffered by individuals
as a result of attempting an exercise referred to in this book. It is strongly
recommended that individuals intending to undertake an exercise program
and any change of diet do so following advice from their doctor.

Photograph credits:
Forza Fitness Equipment Limited,
pages 10, 21, 43, 45, 51, 55, 67, 85,
76, 90, 92 and 93. Nautilus All In
Fitness Limited, pages 48, 83 and 84.
Tylo UK Limited pages 94 and 95.
All other photography © Parragon.

Contents

Introduction
page 6

chapter one
Fit for Life
page 8

chapter two
Training with Weights
page 18

chapter three
Warm Up & Stretch
page 24

chapter four
The Exercises
page 40

chapter five
Using a Fitness Club or Gym
page 80

chapter six
Training for Competition
page 86

chapter seven
Cross Training
page 88

Index of Exercises/Acknowledgements
page 96

Introduction

Fitness generates a feeling of mental and physical well-being. Regular controlled exercise improves physical strength and stamina and creates a level of fitness where energy reserves are high and recovery from fatigue is fast.

Exercise combines strength, stamina and suppleness. It tones the muscles, increases flexibility and improves general health. All-round fitness can be achieved through the controlled tension and relaxation of the muscles during exercise. The following chapters feature exercises which have been selected to improve fitness and build overall strength and stamina.

A body's needs

A body needs energy to move, to work, keep warm and to function correctly. The food we eat and the liquid we drink is capable of providing all the elements required to remain healthy. Our bodies rely on us to make the right dietary choices to provide the necessary nutrients needed for the efficient functioning of all vital body processes.

A complex combination of protein for muscle building, carbohydrates and fats for energy, and vitamins and minerals to keep bones and blood in good repair is essential if we are to become fit and remain healthy.

The importance of a healthy, sensible diet cannot be overlooked if we are to demand greater performance from our bodies as we work to become fitter and achieve an overall feeling of confidence and well-being.

Understanding our body's processes and its dietary requirements will enable us to provide it with the necessary fuel it needs to train to become physically fitter. As our general health and feeling of well-being improves we become increasingly able, both physically and mentally, to cope with the stresses and strains of modern living.

Through regular controlled exercise, sensible eating and relaxation, we can achieve an overall improvement of health which can have a beneficial effect on all aspects of our lives as all vital functions of the body benefit from vigorous activity. Fitness should be a way of life – it should also be fun!

Getting fit

The exercises have been selected to offer a range of movements specifically designed to work the individual muscle groups of the whole body. They are suitable for both men and women, and together with essential warm up and stretch routines, the exercises will enable you to tone the whole body using a range of controlled movements which you can perform at home using free weights.

Many of the movements will also be beneficial to your training without weights, and it is recommended that you perform each exercise without weights until you are familiar with the movements and understand the function of the supporting and active muscles during the exercise.

The use of free weights creates resistance against which the muscles work in the action of lifting or pushing, and this action may also be achieved to an extent, without weights, once the movement is understood and the muscles worked correctly.

Warming up and stretching are a vital part of your routine and these exercises will prepare your body for the demands of your workout, and will relax the muscles following exercise, to avoid possible injury or soreness the following day.

The text guides you through each exercise, and is illustrated with clear step-by-step photographs, and helpful 'Top Tips' become the voice of your personal trainer, guiding you safely and correctly through each movement.

Practical weight training

Training with weights will improve general fitness and body tone. The program you develop can be tailored to your own requirements and need not create increased muscle mass unless desired. The use of light weights combined with a higher number of repetitions will not create bulk but will tone the body and tighten the muscles.

If specific muscle development is required, heavier weights lifted for fewer repetitions will achieve the desired effect and your individual training program can be developed to include the use of resistance machines at your local fitness club, where the qualified staff may offer expert advice. The machines will further develop the movements you have learned at home using free weights.

You may wish to develop your training with weights and progress to bodybuilding, a sport where hard work, strict dietary control, dedication and self-discipline combine to create bodies trained to the very peak of physical development for competition.

Safety first

Safety is of vital importance and cannot be stressed strongly enough.

If you are beginning a training program following illness, if you have a history of coronary heart disease in your family, or if you are particularly overweight or unfit prior to embarking on your new healthy life-style plan, it is important that you consult your doctor and inform him of your intentions.

If you feel unwell or can feel strain on a muscle during exercise, you must stop at once and relax. It is not wise for children who have not stopped growing to work out with weights, and again, your doctor should be consulted and advice taken.

Fit for Life

The energy we need to move comes from chemical reactions in the body. Glucose is 'burned' in the muscles to release energy in the same way that coal releases heat when it is burned as fuel.

The food we eat and the type of exercise we take have a direct influence on our health and general well-being. The human body requires food to build its tissues and to create the energy needed to maintain breathing, heart rate, digestion, growth and repair. Even after we are fully grown and matured, our entire bodies are replaced cell by cell over a period of seven years.

The right fuel

High quality fuel for body maintenance comprising of a careful balance of proteins, fats, carbohydrates, vitamins, minerals, trace elements and water, when combined with exercise to achieve a reasonable level of fitness, will ensure a healthy body, high levels of energy and a general sense of confidence and vitality.

A sensible, healthy diet eating plan need not be monotonous or restricting, or deprive you of your favourite foods forever. A moderate and balanced diet comprising of both the right quality and the right variety of foods will promote good health and generate a feeling of both mental and physical well-being, enabling you to tackle the stresses and strains of every-day life with greater ease and confidence.

A healthy eating program will be noticeable in your appearance. Eat the right fuel and your body will reward you with clear skin, shiny hair, sparkling eyes and an increase in general health and vitality. You really are what you eat, and a gradual change in your eating habits to include fresh fruit and vegetables (high in vitamins and minerals) and low fat sources of protein and carbohydrates, will ensure that your body has the right fuel to create the energy it needs to undertake your fitness program.

Scientific studies have suggested a distinct correlation between high levels of heart disease in Western countries and a modern diet full of processed foods which are high in fat, salt and sugar and low in roughage.

FOOD FACTS

The nutrient value of fruit and vegetables varies according to how they are grown, prepared, cooked and eaten.

◆

Vegetables frozen when at their peak of freshness retain their nutrient value better than those kept in a refrigerator for a few days.

◆

Steam or quickly stir-fry vegetables in a little hot olive oil to preserve their vitamin content.

◆

Take your coolbox to the supermarket to ensure that convenient packs of frozen vegetables are not allowed to thaw on the way home to your own freezer – as re-freezing will damage the vitamin and mineral content.

◆

Aim for at least five portions of different fruit and vegetables per day to ensure an adequate supply of vitamins and minerals.

◆

Saturated fats have been associated with high levels of cholesterol and are mainly found in foods of animal origin, including red meat, milk, butter and cheese.

Dangers of severe dieting

There is no need to change your eating habits overnight. Even if you are overweight, it is not necessary to go on a slimming diet which severely reduces your intake of calories and puts your whole body on starvation alert.

The concept of many weight loss diets is to reduce the total calories eaten per day until they are below the amount of calories burned up by the body as fuel. The theory is that if the fuel is all used up, the body will begin to take its energy from excess fat stored in the tissues – thus causing a reduction in fat and therefore weight loss.

This may at first seem logical, but some medical studies have suggested that the vital body processes react to a deliberate reduction of calories in the same way as they would react in times of famine.

Assuming a starvation situation, your body will adopt survival techniques, lowering the metabolic rate – doing its best not to use up all its fat reserves, and at the first opportunity, i.e. when you begin to return to 'normal' eating, it will over compensate and store up even more fat than it had before – just in case it has to protect itself from a similar famine in the future.

The result could be a vicious circle of continual dieting, weight loss and additional weight gain which is impossible to break until a sensible healthy eating plan is adopted.

FOOD FACTS

Cholesterol is a natural fat-like substance found in the blood and all body tissues. It helps to digest carbohydrates and lubricate arteries and plays an important part in the formation of various cell membranes.

◆

Muscle weighs more than fat. Therefore after a few weeks of exercise your body will be fitter and leaner but may not actually weigh less.

Combined with a healthy diet, exercise will increase muscle and reduce fat. The Body Bar (right) provides an excellent way to improve general body tone at home.

FOOD FACTS

Our food and drink contains every factor necessary for life and health, except the oxygen we breathe.

◆

Women naturally have about 10% more body fat than men.

◆

It is a myth that muscle developed by exercise will turn to fat if the exercise is stopped. Muscle and fat are two completely different things and it is only loss of condition that alters the appearance of the body.

◆

Polyunsaturated fats have been associated with the lowering of blood cholesterol and are found in plants including sunflower, safflower, corn and soya oil, as well as in fish.

◆

In the course of a lifetime, an average person will consume 50 tons of food and 11,000 gallons of liquid.

◆

Sweet corn is a food high in protein and fibre

◆

Eat the right things little and often to prevent hunger pangs.

◆

Exercise will play a large part in re-shaping your body and toning up your muscle and you may discover that you do not need to adopt a weight-loss eating plan after all.

◆

More than 100 different enzymes are involved to digest a meal, breaking down carbohydrates, fats and proteins into nutrients that the individual cells can utilize and use for energy.

◆

Beans, peas and lentils are the edible seeds of leguminous plants. They are a valuable source of protein when combined to provide all the necessary amino acids. They are low in fat and cholesterol and high in fibre.

◆

Cottage cheese is low in fat and high in calcium.

◆

Garlic not only adds flavour to food but thins the blood and aids circulation.

◆

Oven chips contain only half the fat of deep fried chips.

Healthy eating program

The easiest and most beneficial way to change your eating habits is to gradually replace the more undesirable types of food in your diet with healthier alternatives.

◆ It will be easier to continue with your new eating plan if you are not hungry, so always have fruit and vegetables to hand to prevent that empty feeling. Fruit is a good filler – it is full of fibre and water and is a good source of vitamins and carbohydrates for energy. Fresh fruit and raw vegetables will help prevent you resorting, between meals, to a tempting chocolate bar or an apparently healthy cereal bar which has added sugar and hidden calories.

◆ Become familiar with reading ingredients labels, you may be surprised at the hidden sugar and fat content of many ordinary products.

◆ Slowly replace red meat with low fat protein foods such as chicken, fish or a vegetarian bean or soya protein, until you hardly notice it is missing!

◆ Grill or steam foods rather than fry.

◆ Use a low fat vegetable margarine rather than butter.

◆ Use healthy, energy giving cereals rather than those with hidden sugar in the ingredients – if you need a sweetener, add fruit such as bananas or dried fruits or add a little honey.

◆ Use calcium enriched skimmed milk rather than full fat, or use unsweetened soya milk on cereal.

◆ Use low fat cheese instead of the usual full-fat variety.

◆ Use whole grain bread – it is more filling than white bread and is rich in vitamins, minerals and valuable fibre.

◆ Scrub potatoes thoroughly and cook them in their skins for a healthy, filling addition to meals. Potatoes are full of vitamins, carbohydrates and fibre and only fattening when cooked with oil or when butter and cream are added!

◆ Eat fresh fruit for dessert rather than a stodgy pudding.

◆ Drink a glass of clear cool water or unsweetened fruit juice instead of a cup of coffee or a fizzy drink.

◆ If you need a hot drink, try weak black tea without sugar rather than coffee or a milky sweet drink.

◆ Eating between meals is a habit best avoided, but if you feel weak through lack of food, or at times when a quick energy boost is needed to revitalise and give your body strength – perhaps following an exercise session – choose some juicy fresh fruit which is a good source of carbohydrates and will help to replenish lost water.

◆ Banish biscuits, cakes and crisps from your larder – they are only there to tempt you!

◆ Reduce the number of alcoholic drinks consumed at any one time, until one alcoholic drink is enough and eventually you are happy to refrain altogether – except perhaps for the odd drink on special occasions!

FOOD FACTS
Avocado pears are the most nourishing of all fruits, they contain up to 50% oil, 11 vitamins including vitamins A and E, and 14 minerals.
A 7oz (200g) avocado contains approximately 330 calories.

◆

Excessive protein intake can impair vitamin and mineral absorption.

◆

Plant proteins can be combined to provide a complete source of amino acids vital for muscle growth and repair. Choose beans and grains or seeds and legumes to complement each other, even when eaten hours apart at different meals.

◆

Protein should make up about ten percent of the body's food intake.

◆

Monounsaturated fats are now considered even better than polyunsaturated fats in the fight against high levels of cholesterol and are found in olive oil, nuts and avocado pears.

◆

Green plants and some bacteria and algae are the only living things capable of making their own food using the sun's energy in a process called photosynthesis. This is the start of the food chain. Plants are eaten by vegetarian animals who are in turn eaten by carnivores who utilize the sun's energy further up the food chain.

◆

The human body is made up of about 17% protein.

Protein

Approximately one fifth of adult body weight is made up of protein. Protein is a compound composed of amino acids and provides the basic structural properties of cells. It is present in all the structural elements of the body, the muscles which enable the body to move and to work, and the enzymes that carry out the chemical reactions of the digestive system – converting food into useful compounds for the body to utilize. Various types of proteins are required and all are made by the body from those which are taken in the diet.

Proteins are the essential building blocks necessary for body maintenance, the repair of body cells, the growth of new body tissue and the production of the 22 amino acids vital to health. A regular intake of protein is essential as it cannot be stored. Excessive quantities of protein may impede the absorption of minerals and vitamins and it is excreted by the body if it is not required at that time.

Protein is present in most foods in different forms and quantities. Some high protein foods such as red meat, eggs and cheese also contain high levels of fat, whilst others such as beans and peas contain little or no fat. When using red meat, choose lean cuts, trim off visible fat and grill suitable cuts of meat to allow excess fat to drip away. Fish is a valuable source of protein and contains less fat than meat. Nuts are also high in protein but contain quite a high proportion of fat.

Fats

Together with proteins and carbohydrates, fats are one of the three main constituents of food, and are important for a whole range of body functions. Fats are compounds containing glycerol and fatty acids and may be stored in the body until required to provide a valuable source of energy in the form of calories. Fats and oils contain vitamin A and vitamin D which is essential to allow the absorption of calcium vital to healthy bones and teeth. Polyunsaturated fats provide 'essential fatty acids' – substances vital to many body functions.

Whilst an excessive intake of fats and oils may cause a build up of cholesterol in the body and may also lead to weight problems which in turn have a serious effect on health, a totally fat free diet should not be sought as fat is essential for healthy body maintenance.

Cholesterol is associated with fat and is a fat-like substance naturally found in the blood. It plays a vital role in the formation of various cell membranes and lubricates the arteries. It also helps in the digestion of carbohydrates and the absorption of vitamin D.

Over consumption of foods high in saturated fat may lead to excess levels of cholesterol building up in the walls of arteries, which in turn lead to strain on the cardiovascular system and a reduction of oxygen levels within cells throughout the body. Healthy eating and exercise have been shown to assist in the lowering of seriously high cholesterol levels, under medical supervision.

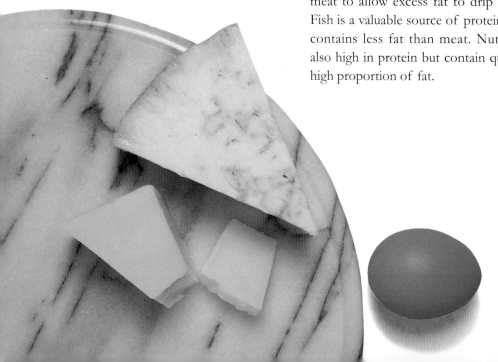

FOOD FACTS
Protein is used by the body to produce amino acids. There are 22 amino acids and all are needed by the body to maintain health. Some cannot be made or converted by the body and therefore must be included in the diet. Eggs contain plentiful amounts of all the amino acids.

Carbohydrates

Carbohydrates provide energy for all the cells in the body. They contain carbon, hydrogen and oxygen which are broken down into glucose which is carried by the bloodstream to its destination. Surplus glucose can by stored in the liver and muscles as glycogen until it is required by the body, when it is then re-converted into glucose. Excessive quantities of glycogen which the liver cannot accommodate will be converted into fat and stored by the body until it is needed as an energy source.

Carbohydrates are the primary fuel for muscle contraction and are the most important nutrient for athletic performance, providing energy to the muscles up to three times as fast as energy obtained from fat.

A diet rich in carbohydrates will replenish energy stores between training sessions as the body's ability to store carbohydrates is limited. Small, frequent meals are a more efficient source of carbohydrate energy than large meals eaten several hours apart, as the body may require a minimum of 20 hours to restore carbohydrate levels exhausted during intense exercise.

Valuable sources of energy giving carbohydrates include pasta, bread, potatoes, rice and other grains. Such foods have previously been considered as stodgy and therefore 'fattening', but it is generally the liberal quantities of oil, butter, cheese and other ingredients eaten with these foods which may result in making them high in fat and unwanted calories.

Vitamins and Minerals

Vitamins are organic substances present in small amounts in most foods, and are essential in varying quantities for the healthy functioning of cells. A sensible, varied diet including a high proportion of fresh fruit and vegetables will ensure a sufficient intake of vitamins, particularly when eaten raw. Cooking will cause some loss of vitamins, reducing the nutrient value of most fresh foods, so it is preferable to eat several pieces of fruit and some vegetables raw – perhaps in the form of a fresh crisp salad – every day.

Eat your greens

Leafy green vegetables are high in vitamin C, folic acid, vitamins E and K and a variety of minerals including iron and calcium. Yellow and orange vegetables such as carrots and most fruits, contain high levels of Vitamin A in the form of carotene.

When preparing vegetables for cooking, do so at the very last minute, exposing the cut surfaces to the air for as little time as possible. Soaking prepared vegetables in water draws out valuable minerals and vitamins which are dissolved and lost. Vegetables should be washed, scrubbed or scraped and peeling should be avoided if possible, as much of the nutrient value of many vegetables is concentrated just under the skin.

Vegetables cooked for a minimum time in a pan with a tight lid, with little or no water, or steamed or pressure cooked for the best results, will yield more goodness, and the cooking water can be used for stock or gravy.

Minerals

Minerals are inorganic substances found in food from both animal and vegetable sources. These substances are made up from the earth, sea and air and although they are required in relatively small quantities, they are essential for the healthy formation of bones, teeth and blood cells, the maintenance of body fluids and the metabolic functions of the body.

A healthy balanced diet will certainly ensure an adequate daily intake of essential minerals. Mineral deficiencies may result in serious side-effects.

Calcium

Calcium forms an essential part of bones and teeth and is important for blood clotting and healthy functioning of the nervous system. The body requires the presence of Vitamin D in the diet to allow efficient absorption of calcium. Dairy products are a valuable source of calcium but are often also high in fat, so low fat varieties of milk, cheese and yogurt are preferable alternatives to full fat varieties.

Dark green vegetables, fortified wholegrain bread and fish such as canned sardines, pilchards and salmon which are eaten with the bones are also high in calcium. A diet deficient in calcium may result in brittle bones and weak teeth.

Calcium deficiency can contribute to the onset of osteoporosis in women following menopause. Muscle cramps during exercise may indicate a lack of sufficient calcium in the diet.

Pumping iron

Iron is needed in the manufacture of haemoglobin, the oxygen-carrying compound in the blood. It is stored in the liver and carried to bone marrow as it is required. Foods rich in iron include red meat products with a high blood content, particularly liver.

Iron is most readily absorbed by the human body from red meat sources and it is also present in egg yolk, oysters, raisins, chocolate, molasses and dried apricots. Iron requires the presence of vitamin C in the diet to allow efficient absorption. Deficiency is related to anaemia, the initial symptom of which is fatigue – it may also cause dizziness and palpitations. Women lose iron through menstruation but are likely to be aware of the importance of iron in the diet. Often, foods with a high iron content are craved when levels are low.

Fibre

Fibre is the collective word used to describe the substances found in the walls of plant cells. Fibre, or roughage is present in all natural plant foods in the form of cellulose. It is not digested or absorbed by the body but assists digestion by giving 'bulk' to the food eaten, enabling it to pass through the digestive system smoothly. A lack of dietary fibre may result in constipation and other more serious diseases of the digestive system.

The best sources of dietary fibre are wholegrain cereals – particularly bran, vegetables, fruit and nuts. Wholegrain bread and pasta, brown rice, beans, lentils and cereals contain high levels of fibre and are also high in minerals and vitamins and very low in fat. Processed foods, white bread, white rice and white pasta are made with cereals which have had the fibre removed and therefore contain little or no fibre.

Fibre provides a satisfying bulk to meals without added fat or calories. A simple way to increase fibre intake is to eat fruit and vegetables complete with the skins which are high in fibre.

Always ensure fruit and vegetables are carefully washed to eliminate traces of pesticides used in growing. Organic fruit and vegetables are grown without the use of chemicals and are generally considered to be healthier.

Nutrient	Sources	Needed for
Vitamin A	Fish, eggs, butter, margarine, milk cheese, liver, beetroot, artichokes cabbage, lettuce, chicken, beef, lamb	Necessary for normal vision, protects against bacterial infection and protects skin.
Vitamin D	Eggs, butter, margarine, cheese, oily fish, natural sunlight	Aids calcium absorption Needed for bones and teeth
B Complex (Vitamins B1 B2, B3, B5, B6 B12)	Yeast, liver, pork, cereals, beans, peas, nuts, kidney, lamb, pork, beef, leeks, spinach, parsnips, celery, broccoli, milk, fruit, potatoes, bananas	Required for correct functioning of the brain, digestive and nervous systems and for healthy skin, hair, eyes, mouth and liver. Protects against mild depression and anaemia.
Vitamin C	Blackcurrant, broccoli, oranges, lemons apples, carrots, all green vegetables, potatoes, tomatoes, peppers, cod, rose hips	Assists growth and repair of cells and tissues and fights infection. Essential for efficient absorption of iron
Biotin	Egg yolks, liver, kidney, oatflakes, wheatbran, wheatgerm, wholemeal bread, brown rice, whole grains	Important in the utilization of carbohydrates, fats and proteins, for energy and protects against stress-induced effects
Calcium	Milk, cheese, eggs, butter, bread, spinach	For growth and repair of bones and teeth, transmission of nerve impulses, controlling cholesterol and ensuring normal heart function and absorption of B12
Iron	Meat, liver, eggs, broccoli, spinach, cereals, brussels sprouts, cauliflower	Vital for the transportation of oxygen in the blood to muscles
Folic Acid	Liver, oranges, milk, asparagus, meat, leeks, green leafy vegetables	Vital for healthy blood and the breakdown of nutrients in food
Zinc	Fish, seafood, meat, wholegrains, seeds, pulses, root vegetables	Used in all vital body functions particularly mental activity and sexual function, also assists the senses of taste and smell
Selenium	Yeast, meat, fish, seafood, cereals, dairy products, fruit, vegetables	Aids vitamin absorption and protects against disease

Sugar

It is well known that sugar is bad for teeth and likely to result in weight gain if eaten in large quantities, but it is still considered a good source of immediate energy and often used, perhaps in the form of a chocolate bar as a quick 'pick-me-up' to give instant energy.

Simple natural sugars in the form of glucose and fructose found in sweet and dried fruits provide immediate energy, as they are absorbed directly into the blood without the need for digestive enzymes.

Sugar provides energy in the form of 'empty' calories, so called because it provides no other food value. There are no vitamins or minerals in sugar and the body does not need sugar in order to function, as it makes its own sugar for energy from carbohydrate sources.

Studies suggest that communities with a high intake of sugar in the diet show a higher incidence of coronary heart disease, obesity and diabetes. Sugar in its most obvious forms might be easy to avoid, but many hidden sugars are present in the most unexpected foods, so it is wise to read the labels of prepared foods.

Salt

Salt is present in most foods. It is responsible for maintaining the correct osmotic pressure of the blood and tissue fluids, and is involved in muscle activity. Salt is lost from the body through perspiration. Severe loss of salt may result in a dramatic fall in blood pressure, cramps, apathy and vomiting.

High levels of salt are present in many processed foods including hard cheese, bread, cereals, processed meats, fish and bacon and it is often added to cooking as a habit. Decreasing salt intake has been shown to help reduce blood pressure.

Water

The human body is composed of over two-thirds water. It is required by all body cells and makes all body functions and processes possible. Fluid lost through the removal of waste from the body must be replaced throughout the day, and it is recommended that at least 1.7 litres (3 pints) of fluid is taken every day – although much more will be needed if you are fitness training and losing extra fluids through sweat.

Mild dehydration may result in loss of energy and constipation, but serious dehydration can cause death. The human body can survive several days without food, but only four days without water.

While you are exercising it is important to take sips of water, fruit juice or a glucose drink to replace the fluids lost through sweat. If you deny your body fluids during an energetic work-out you may cause temporary dehydration which is damaging to your body. If you feel thirsty during or after exercise, it is already too late – you have begun to dehydrate.

Sweating is the body's natural temperature regulating mechanism and a way of excreting waste products. It is made up of about 1 per cent urea and salt and 99 per cent water. Salt in the body also regulates sweating and if there is too little salt present in the body, too much water will be lost and dehydration may occur. During exercise the body's temperature rises and when it reaches 37.4 degrees C (99.3 degrees F), three million tiny glands begin to produce sweat.

Food, as well as drink is a valuable source of water and foods with a high water content are often also high in fibre. A large part of your daily fluid intake should be in the form of fresh water and fruit juices. Alcohol, coffee and tea are diuretics and encourage fluid loss. The body does not need caffeine, which is a stimulant found in both tea and coffee, and caffeine-free products are now widely available. Studies have suggested, however, that tea contains vitamin-like properties that may play a role in preventing heart disease, together with substances which actually enhance the action of vitamin C.

FOOD FACTS

Did you know that a serving of baked beans can contain as much sugar as approximately one and a half chocolate digestive biscuits?

◆

There may be between 10-12 teaspoonfuls of sugar in a can of soft drink.

◆

Every living cell within the body relies on water to dissolve compounds and enable essential chemicals to be exchanged.

◆

The body is made up of about 60 – 70% water – as much as ten gallons (38 litres).

◆

An adult requires more than 3 pints (1.7 litres) of fluid per day.

◆

Alcohol, tea and coffee are diuretics – they promote fluid loss, and therefore are not ideal fluids to replenish the body following exercise.

◆

Wash canned tuna to remove salty brine.

When choosing a fruit juice, be sure you are getting the real thing. Some fruit juices may only be one third real juice with sugar water added.

QUIZ

How healthy are your present eating habits? Tick the boxes and answer **YES** or **NO** to the following questions:

HEALTHY EATING CHECKLIST A

	YES	NO
Do you eat red meat more than 2 or 3 times per week?	☐	☐
Do you eat less than 3 meals per day?	☐	☐
Do you miss breakfast but eat a large meal late at night?	☐	☐
Do you add salt to your food?	☐	☐
Do you eat sugary or high fat snacks between meals?	☐	☐
Do you drink more than 4 cups of coffee per day?	☐	☐
Do you feel the need to 'diet' from time to time?	☐	☐
Do you prefer a can of fizzy drink to a glass of water?	☐	☐
Do you eat when you are bored or depressed?	☐	☐
Do you drink alcohol most days or in large quantities?	☐	☐

HEALTHY EATING CHECKLIST B

	YES	NO
Do you eat a healthy breakfast?	☐	☐
Do you eat 3 regular meals per day?	☐	☐
Do you drink at least 4 glasses of water per day?	☐	☐
Do you eat fish, chicken or vegetable protein in preference to red meat?	☐	☐
Do you limit your alcohol consumption to one or two occasions per week?	☐	☐
Do you drink less than 4 cups of coffee per day?	☐	☐
Do you include fresh fruit and vegetables at every meal?	☐	☐
Do you limit your consumption of foods high in fat?	☐	☐
Do you limit your consumption of foods high in sugar?	☐	☐
Do you read the labels of prepared foods and avoid those containing too many chemical additives?	☐	☐

Have you ticked more **YES's** in *CHECKLIST A* than *B*? If so, you may need to begin to gradually change your present eating habits in favour of a healthier eating program.

If you have ticked more **YES's** in *CHECKLIST B*, you seem to be aware that your body requires the correct fuel for health and fitness, but to which questions did you tick **NO**? There may still be room for further improvement.

Training with Weights

Well developed chest and back muscles will give you a broad shouldered, narrow-waisted appearance and contribute to an upright posture which will also help to avoid backache.

These exercises have been selected to introduce you to the basics of working out with weights. The aim of each exercise is to work a particular muscle group, and the basic movements are those upon which most controlled exercises are based.

Each exercise works specific muscles, working from head to foot. Once these controlled movements are mastered, and as you become increasingly fitter, you will gradually be able to increase the number of exercises undertaken in a single session, enabling you to progress and increase the weights lifted with safety and confidence.

Many of these exercises may be performed using the latest equipment at a fitness club or gym, where the basic movements you have learned may be further developed and the weights lifted safely increased under professional supervision.

The muscle groups

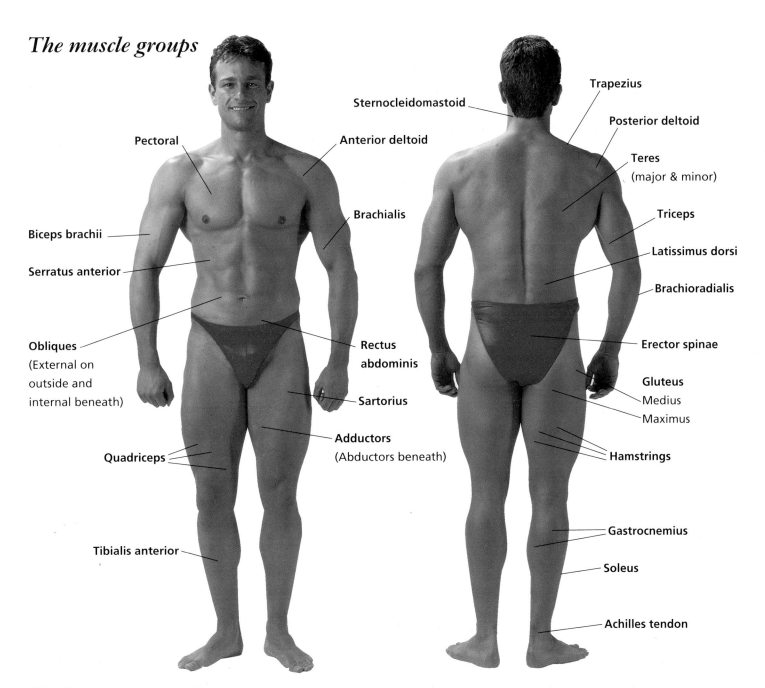

Front view labels:
- Pectoral
- Biceps brachii
- Serratus anterior
- Obliques (External on outside and internal beneath)
- Quadriceps
- Tibialis anterior
- Sternocleidomastoid
- Anterior deltoid
- Brachialis
- Rectus abdominis
- Sartorius
- Adductors (Abductors beneath)

Back view labels:
- Trapezius
- Posterior deltoid
- Teres (major & minor)
- Triceps
- Latissimus dorsi
- Brachioradialis
- Erector spinae
- Gluteus Medius Maximus
- Hamstrings
- Gastrocnemius
- Soleus
- Achilles tendon

Understand your body

The human body contains 650 voluntary muscles attached to the skeleton by means of tough 'elastic bands' of tissue called tendons.

Muscles assist posture and enable the body to stand upright, balance and move. Fit muscles allow greater mobility and flexibility and well developed muscles make a body strong and agile.

Muscles become increasingly flexible with exercise and although they are generally tolerant of the demands made upon them, they are not individually strong and are easily damaged if care is not taken to warm up, stretch and cool down when exercising. Muscles allow our joints to move as levers and assist the organs of the body in their functions.

Flexor muscles bend a limb at the joint like a lever, and opposing muscles known as extensors straighten the limb. It is therefore vital to exercise and strengthen opposing muscles to ensure balance, as muscles can only pull, they cannot push.

Muscles have many functions – chest muscles contract and relax to help empty and fill the lungs with air, flexor muscles in the forearm bend the wrist and fingers, biceps and triceps bend and straighten the arm.

Developing and strengthening the muscles can increase overall physical and mental health and fitness, improve heart rate and respiration and change the shape of the body. Care must be taken to provide the muscles with the appropriate fuel to provide the energy required to function correctly, and to understand the capabilities and limitations of the human body, in order to avoid overstressing muscles and risking injury.

Beginning to train

All bodies respond to physical training, and it is important to consider your own level of fitness and health before embarking on a strenuous fitness program.

If you have not taken any exercise for some time, or if you have suffered ill health of any kind, it is very important that you consult your doctor, particularly if you have a personal or family history of heart trouble or high blood pressure.

Remember, as you start to train, always listen to your body. Do not over-train, and take care not to over stress your body if suffering from a cold or any other illness.

Repetitions

As a guide, an exercise or movement should be repeated a number of times to obtain the maximum benefit and a given number of repetitions are suggested for each exercise.

Ten repetitions should be suitable in the early stages of your weight training program, but if you feel that this is over stressful for your particular level of fitness, reduce the repetitions to five until you feel that you can safely undertake more.

As your level of fitness increases, you will be able to incorporate a greater number of different exercises performed in a single session and be able to increase the number of repetitions of each exercise.

A good guide to the progress of your training is that once you are easily able to do 10 repetitions of an exercise, it is time to undertake more repetitions, or increase the weight lifted or the dumbbell size.

It is important to remember that you are aiming to work the whole body, so you should only increase the weights once you can perform all the exercises with ease. This will be a good indicator of your progress.

Muscle Tone

If you are exercising to build up muscle mass, greater benefit will be achieved with fewer repetitions using heavier weights. If you are exercising to become generally fitter and to tone up the whole body, then between 10 and 15 repetitions of each exercise will be more beneficial, even if the weights lifted remain relatively light.

As you become fitter you will want to work out for longer and increase your exercise program. This can be achieved by performing 'sets' each designed to work separate areas of the body, gradually increasing the number of repetitions.

Remember to rest in between each set of repetitions to avoid over stressing the muscles and risk injury.

Stay with it

Once you have chosen a program of exercises to work all areas of the body, try to stay with your choice until you find 10 repetitions of each exercise easy in a single session.

The Cybex AB Trainer, above, works the same muscles as crunch sit ups, see page 72.

Consistency is the best way to achieve results, so do not be tempted to abandon certain exercises and therefore neglect particular areas of the body in favour of others. By all means add more challenging exercises to your program as you progress but do not neglect particular muscle groups if you find the exercises difficult.

Set yourself a goal each week and be determined to achieve it. A good way to make sure you stick to your program each week is to work out with a partner who can assist with the more difficult exercises and who will offer mutual support and encouragement.

You will soon find that you are increasing your program, performing greater numbers of repetitions and lifting heavier weights when you have the added element of friendly competition with a companion.

Ten Safety Rules to Remember

1   Start all standing exercises with your feet shoulder width apart

2   Concentrate on the exercise, do not allow yourself to be distracted – this is your time to exercise and you should concentrate on the movements and rhythm of the exercises

3   Do not arch your back. Your spine supports you at all times and must be strong and firm to avoid injury. When lifting heavy weights it is wise to wear a weight lifting support belt to protect your back. Ask your sports supplier or fitness club staff for advice

4   Always control the movement of the exercise, do not jerk the weights

5   Remember to breathe out on the exertion of the exercise and to breathe in when returning to the starting position

6   Do not try to lift more weight than is sensible – gradually increase the weights as your muscles become fitter and more capable of taking the strain

7   Always try to give yourself 24 hours rest between exercise sessions

8   Always warm up and warm down thoroughly to avoid injury

9   Always keep your head up and your chin straight to assist with balance. It is often said that where your eyes look – your body will follow

10 Never continue to work out if you become dizzy or feel fatigued, or suspect you may have strained a muscle. Injury may result in working an over-stressed muscle, or one which is insufficiently warmed up

The Equipment

The equipment required to begin weight training at home is available from good sports shops.

As you begin to work out using weights, you may start with a single set of dumbbells and perhaps a bench, and gradually add different pieces of equipment to your collection as your training program progresses and your fitness increases.

Equipment can be costly, and it is advisable to buy the best equipment that you can afford, but by shopping around or purchasing 'nearly-new', you will be able to set up your very own gym at home within your budget.

When buying larger items, such as exercise bicycles or rowing machines to assist with your cross-training, always take the time to try out different models to ensure you buy the one which suits and 'fits' you.

Barbell
Check that the length of the bar is suitable for your height and arm-span. Choose the correct length which feels comfortable to you and ask the advice of an experienced friend or the shop assistant before making your choice.

Dumbbells
Be sure to choose a set which allows adjustment of the disc weights. A set of light dumbbells are ideal for the beginner, and will help to build confidence in the movements before progressing to heavier weights.

Hand held weights
Can be useful if you wish to get used to using weights before progressing to dumbbells or a barbell.

Push up handles
Good for taking the strain off your wrists when performing press ups. Particularly useful if the chest is an area you are specifically interested in developing.

Ankle Weights
Where possible, choose those which have adjustable straps to ensure a comfortable fit, and removable individual weights for versatility.

Bench
Check that the bench is sturdy and stable. Try it out to see if it takes your weight without feeling unsteady. Is it large enough for you, and will it fit into your exercise area at home?

Wrist Weights
Ensure they fit your wrists comfortably. They should not be so tight that they restrict blood circulation, but neither should they be too large and risk slipping off during training.

Step

Check that the step is sturdy and does not rock when you stand on it. Make sure it is large enough to allow you to step up with confidence without looking down and has removable risers to allow you to adjust the height.

Workout mat

Choose one which is large enough for your requirements. There are many different designs on the market to suit all budgets.

Rebounder

A great investment towards your general fitness program, a rebounder will allow you to jog without leaving the house and will enable you to enjoy aerobic exercise without putting unnecessary stress on knees or muscles recovering from injury.

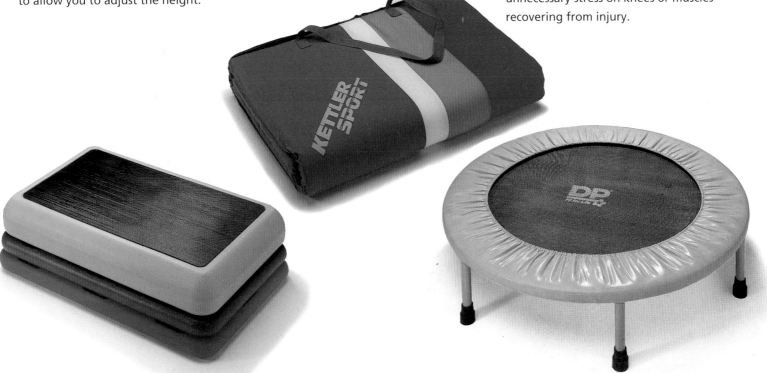

Clothes

Suitable clothes for sports and training are widely available and the style chosen is very much personal choice. Clothes should be loose and comfortable, made of fabrics which will breathe and must be able to withstand regular washing.

Some sports manufacturers make clothes which are specially designed with particular activities in mind and it is advisable to buy the best quality you can afford if you are to train regularly. Wear layers of light, loose-fitting clothes for maximum flexibility.

Training Indoors

Shorts and vest is ideal for both men and women for working inside and outside in warm weather. Women may prefer a loose leotard with leggings or an all-in-one dance tunic. A supporting sports or 'bounce' bra is essential for women. Keep a sweat-shirt or tracksuit

to hand to slip on following a workout to avoid chills.

Training Outdoors

A loose-fitting warm tracksuit will be the ideal basis for your outdoor clothing, with a cotton tee-shirt worn next to the skin. A water- and wind-proof jacket with a hood is a must for jogging or cycling outside in all weathers and you may find gloves comfortable in very cold weather.

Pockets in your jacket or trousers will be useful for carrying your keys and personal alarm etc.

Shoes

Training shoes are the most important item of clothing that you will buy. They absorb impact and protect your feet, legs and back from injury. Care should be taken to choose the correct shoe for

the activity and the highest quality you can afford. Buy from a reputable sports stockist and ask the advice of the staff to ensure you make the right choice.

Shoes designed for a particular activity have specific cushioning, absorbing and supporting qualities in particular areas, and will not be entirely suitable for other activities. It may therefore be necessary to invest in more than one pair of quality training shoes for all aspects of your training.

Buy shoes at the end of the day, when your feet are warm and have expanded. It will be some time before new shoes feel really comfortable, so it is wise to begin wearing them for short periods, keeping your previous shoes in reserve for comfort. New shoes which begin feeling too soft will not give the support required for safety and comfort and will soon lose their shape.

Warm Up & Stretch

Just 15-20 minutes of exercise, three times per week gives 30 per cent fitness improvement – even a brisk walk will improve your fitness.

Warming up and stretching is a very important part of your workout routine and is essential to avoid injuries. Your warm up routine should increase your heart-rate and relax your muscles. You can do this by jogging outside, on the spot, on a rebounder, with a skipping rope, or by cycling – outside or using a static exercise bicycle.

You may choose any one of these methods or enjoy a combination of two or more. Warming up gets your body ready for the training session, and it is important that every part of the body is warmed up and stretched sufficiently to enable your muscles to perform during exercise.

Once you have warmed up, stretching will relax both your mind and your body, preparing you mentally for the workout to follow. Ensure that you warm up enough to avoid putting undue stress on your muscles and connective tissue as you stretch. Stretching should be slow and controlled and is also an ideal way to cool down and relax your body after your workout, to relax your body following the stress of working out.

REMEMBER

◆ Warming up is as important to your exercise programme as the individual exercises themselves

◆ Warming up will help to prevent injuries

◆ Warming up prepares your muscles for the stresses of exercise

◆ Warming up increases your heart rate and improves circulation

◆ Warming up and stretching relaxes your muscles and limbers up your joints

◆ Don't be tempted to skimp on your warm up routine

◆ Warm up every part of the body, particularly those areas on which you wish to concentrate

◆ Stretching relaxes mind and body

◆ Stretching should be slow and controlled

◆ Do not bounce or move quickly when stretching

◆ Stretch to the limit, but not to the point that it is painful

◆ Hold your stretch for 20 seconds or more and then release slowly

◆ Stretching should be graceful and gradual, with slow fluid movements

◆ Remember that correct breathing is essential

Turns

Stand with feet slightly apart, arms straight down by your sides, shoulders square.

Turn your head from side to side as far as you can.

Perform the movement in a controlled, balanced rhythm.

Repeat the exercise 10 times.

Muscles worked: Sternocleidomastoids

TOP TIPS

◆ **Do not move your head from side to side too fast**

◆ **Remember to control the movement**

BODY TALK

Muscles are a collection of long narrow cells called fibres which can contract. The muscles are attached to bones by elastic tissue called tendons.

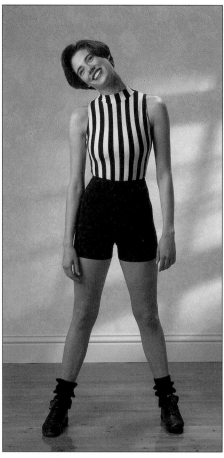

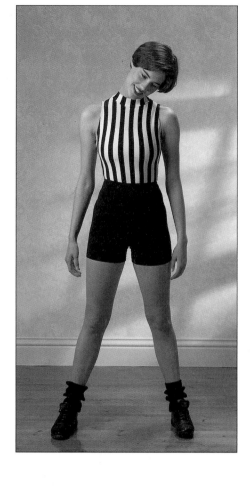

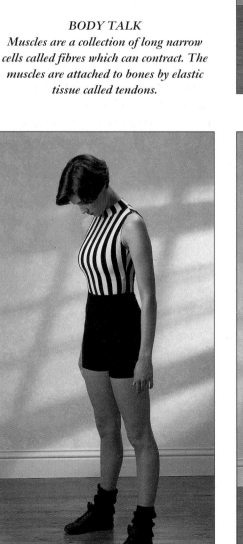

Nods

Stand with feet slightly apart. Arms should be relaxed and by your side with shoulders square.

Roll your head gently forwards, and then backwards, returning to the upright position.

Repeat the exercise 10 times.

Muscles worked: Sternocleidomastoids

TOP TIPS

◆ **Do not hunch your shoulders**

◆ **Be relaxed and move your neck only**

◆ **Always keep your eyes open**

◆ **Never throw your head backwards to stretch the back of your neck**

Arm Raise Front

Stand with feet slightly apart, shoulders square.

With arms at waist height, link your hands together in front of your body.

Raise your arms slowly above your head. Inhale deeply as you raise your arms through the movement.

Exhale as you return to the starting position.

Muscles worked: Posterior deltoids, latissimus dorsi, obliques

TOP TIPS
◆ **Do not lean forward – keep your back straight at all times**
◆ **Keep your head straight with your view fixed to one point**

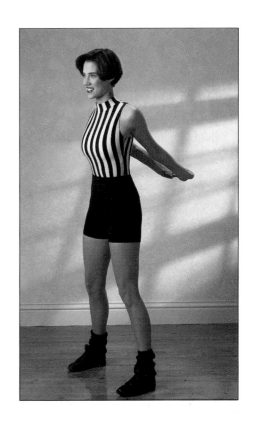

Arm Raise Back

Stand with your feet slightly apart with shoulders square.

With your arms by your side, link your hands together behind your back. Inhale as you raise your linked arms together as high as they will go.

Exhale as you return to the starting position keeping your hands locked together behind you.

Repeat both exercises 10 times.

Muscles worked: Posterior deltoids, latissimus dorsi, obliques

Side Bends

Stand with your feet shoulder width apart.

Interlock your hands behind your head, with elbows pointing out to each side.

Bend from the waist, side to side, keeping the upper body straight and the hips square.

Repeat the exercise 10 times on each side.

Muscles worked: *Latissimus dorsi, external obliques*

TOP TIP

◆ **Remember to keep the hips still at all times**

FITNESS FACT
Massage can bring many benefits to tired muscles following strenuous exercise, relaxing both the body and the mind.

Torso Circles

Stand with your feet turned slightly out – about three feet apart.

Place your hands on your hips. Keeping your hips square and still, bend forwards from the waist, then back to the centre position.

Bend to the right, then back to the central position, and then to the left in turn.

Repeat this movement 5 times, and then reverse direction.

Muscles worked: *Latissimus dorsi, external obliques*

TOP TIP

◆ **Keep the movement smooth and maintain a rhythm**

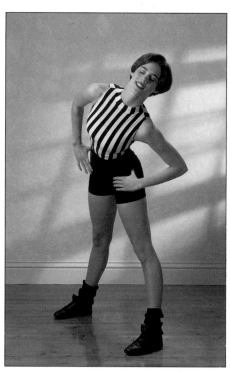

Straight Overs

Stand with your feet shoulder width apart, body straight and relaxed.

Slowly lower your head and roll your body forward vertebrae by vertebrae, as far as you can.

See if you can go all the way and touch your feet or the floor in front of you with your hands.

Slowly raise your body gradually to the original standing position.

Remember do not to over strain, let your body build up to the exercise.

Muscles worked: Gluteus, latissimus dorsi, hamstrings

TOP TIP
◆ Do not be tempted to bounce to reach the floor, greater flexibility will come as your body becomes fitter

WARNING if you have any lower back problems, you should avoid this exercise

Hip Swings – Backwards and Forwards

This exercise may be performed wearing leg weights, once you have mastered the movements.

Using a chair or another solid structure, place your left hand on your hip, balancing with the right hand on the back of the chair.

Swing your left leg forward and backwards several times in a smooth rhythmic movement.

Repeat 10 times.

Swing your leg from side to side in front of your body.

Repeat 10 times.

Now change legs and repeat the exercise.

Muscles worked: Hamstrings, Quadriceps

Swings – Side to Side

As above but swing your leg from side to side, crossing in front of your body.

Repeat 10 times for each leg

TOP TIPS
◆ Keep your back as straight as possible
◆ Keep your head up and fix your eyes on a point in the room to assist your balance

Side Lunges

Stand with your feet in a wide stance, and place your hands on your hips.

Dip your hips to one side, then the other.

Remember to keep your feet still.

You should control the movement in a slow rhythm.

Do not move fast from side to side as this could cause muscle strain.

This exercise may also be performed wearing leg weights

Muscles worked: Gluteus maximus, hamstrings

TOP TIPS

◆ **Remember – do not lean forward**

◆ **Keep your head straight**

BODY TALK

Muscles can only pull – they cannot push. Each moveable joint needs two muscles, one to pull and one to pull back.

◆

The carbon in glucose is combined with oxygen in the muscles and carried by the blood where it forms carbon dioxide, which is then expelled by the lungs.

Lifts

Using a chair, or another suitable structure, place one hand out to assist your balance.

Stand on the balls of your feet, body straight, right arm by your side.

Lower and lift your heels several times, keeping your feet parallel.

Repeat the exercise 10 times.

BODY TALK
Muscle and skin cells continue to grow and reproduce throughout our lives, but brain cells and nerve cells die and are not replaced.

To work all areas of the calf muscle you can also do the same exercise turning your toes out – and then in – in order to get the full benefit of the exercise.

Muscles worked: *Gastrocnemius, soleus*

Remember to include a stretching session during your warm up and following your workout. Stretching during your warm up will help to relax your muscle groups, and after your workout it will help disperse the lactic acids in the muscles and prevent soreness the following day.

You must always warm up your body before you stretch to ensure you do not put undue stress on the muscles you are about to use.

When stretching, remember to move through the exercise in a slow and controlled movement and be careful not to bounce. Take each stretching movement to the limit but not to the extreme where it becomes painful as this could be dangerous.

Remember to inhale deeply while stretching and hold the final position for 20 seconds, then slowly exhale as you gradually return to the starting position through a controlled movement.

Neck Stretch

Stand with your feet shoulder width apart.

Extend your left arm sideways at shoulder height with palm upwards.

Place your right ear as close to your right shoulder as possible and slowly bring your left hand up and over your head, placing your hand against your right ear.

Pull gently and hold for a few seconds. Repeat exercise with right arm extended.

Repeat ten times each side.

Muscles worked: *Medial deltoids, Sternocleidomastoids*

Shoulder Curls

Stand with your feet shoulder width apart.

Place your hands on top of your shoulders with elbows pointing out to each side.

Now, with your elbows make large circles in the air – ten forwards, and ten backwards.

Muscles worked: *Posterior deltoids, latissimus dorsi*

TOP TIP
◆ **Keep your back straight and look forward**

Head Rolls

Stand with your feet shoulder width apart. Place both hands behind your neck and lean head backwards.

Keep your back straight and knees slightly bent.

Gently press your head forward onto your chest and hold for 4-8 seconds.

Repeat 10 times.

Muscles worked: *Medial deltoids, Sternocleidomastoids*

Rib Stretching – Forwards

Stand in an open doorway and grasp the doorframes with each hand just below shoulder height.

   Slowly lean forward, straighten your arms and support your weight with each hand.

   Hold for 20 seconds and slowly return to the straight position.

   Repeat 10 times.

Muscles worked: Posterior deltoids, Trapezius, triceps

Rib Stretching – Backwards

Standing in the doorway, repeat the exercise, but this time lean backwards. Repeat 10 times.

Muscles worked: Posterior deltoids, Trapezius, triceps

BODY TALK

The major chemical elements of the body include hydrogen, oxygen, nitrogen, carbon, calcium, magnesium, sodium, potassium, chlorine, sulphur and iron.

◆

All living things are made up of carbon in various forms. The human body contains enough carbon to fill about 9,000 lead pencils and enough phosphorus to make 2,200 matches.

Side Stretches

Stand with your feet shoulder width apart.

Begin with both arms raised above your head and hold your left wrist with your right hand.

Gently pull to the right as far as you can.

Ensure that your back remains straight, allowing your torso to bend whilst keeping your hips square and still.

Repeat 10 times each side.

Muscles worked: Latissimus dorsi, obliques

Seated Side Stretches

Sit on the floor with your legs in a 'V' position, keeping your back as straight as possible.

Point your right foot and rest your right forearm on your right thigh.

Keeping your left hip on the floor and your left shoulder as straight as possible, bring your left arm up and over your head and stretch to touch your right toe.

Hold for 3 seconds and return slowly to the upright position.

Remember to exhale through the movement and inhale as you return.

Repeat 10 times each side.

Muscles worked: External obliques

TOP TIP

◆ **Do not lean too far forward – hold the shoulders back to allow the chest to 'open'**

FITNESS FACT
Breathing properly is essential for the correct functioning of the heart and for successful exercising.

Torso Stretches

Stand with your feet shoulder width apart.

With both elbows at shoulder height, pointing out to the sides, grasp your right wrist with your left hand.

Pull your right arm across the front of your body as far as you can and hold.

Keep shoulders square and back straight at all times.

Repeat 10 times each side.

Muscles worked: Latissimus dorsi, obliques

Front Hip Stretch

From a standing position, bend your knees and lower your body down until you can place both hands flat on the floor in front of you at shoulder width.

Rest your right knee on the floor and then extend the leg backwards until it is almost straight.

The left leg remains under the body, with ankle and knee aligned at 90 degrees to the floor.

Push your right hip gently towards the floor until you can feel the stretch.

Hold and exhale.

Repeat 10 times on each side.

Muscles worked: Sartorius, quadriceps

Scissors

Lay on your back and lift your legs straight up at 90 degree to the floor.

Open your legs as far as possible making a wide 'V' shape.

Place each hand on your inner thigh and gently press to increase the stretch.

Muscles worked: Adductors

TOP TIP
◆ **Keep the head straight and do not be tempted to raise the head or chest to assist the stretch**

Below: Front hip stretch and scissors

Butterflies

Sit on the floor with your back straight, knees bent out sideways, and the soles of the feet together.

Bring your heels as close to your body as possible, place your hands on the floor behind you for balance and gently press your knees towards the floor.

Repeat 10 times.

Muscles worked: *Adductors*

TOP TIP

◆ Do not bounce your knees – make sure the movement is controlled throughout.

◆ Bouncing may cause injury to the inner thigh muscles

Cross-Legged Stretch

Sit on the floor with your legs crossed.

Extend your arms forwards in front of your body and place elbows and hands on the floor.

Press forward and hold for 5 seconds.

Exhale as you press forward and inhale as you slowly return to the starting position.

Muscles worked: *Gluteus maximus*

Thigh Stretch

Using the back of a chair or another solid structure, stand on your right leg, balancing with your right hand.

Standing straight, reach back with your left hand and grasp your left foot, pulling it as close as possible to your buttocks.

Hold and breathe.

Repeat 10 times for each leg.

Muscles worked: *Quadriceps*

TOP TIPS

◆ **Keep knees together to improve the stretch and maintain balance**

◆ **Keep your head up and fix your eyes on a point in the room**

FITNESS FACT
Regular exercise strengthens the heart, lowers blood pressure and reduces stress.

Ankle Roll

Sit in a chair with your right foot on the floor.

Cross your left leg over in front and support the calf on your right knee.

With your right hand, hold your left foot and rotate it in circles several times in each direction.

Repeat with right foot.

Muscles worked: *Achilles tendon*

TOP TIP

◆ **Let your hand do the work to allow your ankle to relax**

FITNESS FACT
A cold shower should not be taken just after exercise – have a warm shower first and a cold shower once your body temperature has reduced and heart rate has slowed.

Ham String Stretch

Extend your right leg and support the foot on a chair or other suitable structure so that it is parallel to the floor.

Hold your right shin with both hands and slowly press your chest towards the extended leg until you feel the stretch.

Hold for 3 seconds.

Repeat 10 times for each leg.

Muscles worked: Hamstrings, adductors, erector spinae

TOP TIP

◆ **If you have lower back problems, do not press your chest forward, but dip the standing leg to achieve the same stretch**

Wall Stretches

Facing a wall, place your hands flat against the wall at shoulder height.

Lean forward and support your weight.

Place your feet as far back as you can, keeping your heels flat on the floor.

Hold until you feel the stretch.

Muscles worked: Hamstrings, gluteus maximus, gastrocnemius, soleus, achilles tendon

TOP TIP

◆ **Feet must always be flat on the floor with the heels together**

BODY TALK
Sunbathing may make us feel good, but too much exposure to the sun's ultraviolet light is potentially harmful.
The body creates a defence mechanism in response to the electromagnetic radiation emitted by the sun and triggers the production of melanin in the skin which causes tanning. Too much sun overloads the body's systems leading to sunburn and even cancer.

Stretch it out

There are many ways to stretch your body following a workout.

Make sure you can feel the stretch, hold briefly and rest for a few moments before working on a different area.

Buttock stretch

Lower back stretch

General back stretch

Lower back stretch

The Exercises

The following selection of exercises are intended to introduce you to training at home using free weights – dumbbells and barbells.

If you have never worked out using weights, it is recommended that you try the exercises without weights before progressing to light dumbbells, to ensure that the movements are being followed through correctly and safely.

Leg and wrist weights may also be used once the movements have been mastered. It is very important to control the movements and to avoid making sudden moves, as the joints of the limb may be pulled by the force of the added weight, risking injury.

The exercises will be beneficial to your fitness training without the use of weights. This will give you confidence in the movement, allowing you to feel the muscles working and experience the rhythm of the movements, before progressing to the next stage.

Overall Fitness

Working out at home with free weights provides many varied opportunities for improving the general level of body tone and the overall fitness of all muscle groups. It is vital to ensure that all of the major muscle groups are worked at each session.

Each muscle group is influenced and assisted by other groups, and these groups will also require strengthening, to ensure that the exercises are performed safely and effectively.

Once the movements have been mastered using light weights, the weight may be increased, or a barbell used instead of dumbbells, where appropriate.

It may be a good idea to ask a friend to train with you, so that you can assist each other with the heavier weights and correct each other's position where necessary, to gain the most benefit from the movements. Working out in front of a mirror will also help you to achieve the correct position for each exercise.

Increased Strength

As you train with weights, your muscles will become stronger and your general body tone will improve.

Weight training, even with light weights will improve general fitness and muscle tone. It will only add noticeable bulk to your muscles if your personal training program is designed to do so.

Performing fewer repetitions using increasingly heavier weights will add muscle mass and increase overall strength (see Developing a Personal Training Program, page 74).

The selected exercises will introduce you to the basic movements performed when working the major muscle groups. These same movements may then be developed further with the use of the latest gym equipment at your local fitness club, where you may progress your training with the added benefit of advice and assistance from the qualified staff.

Warm Up and Cool Down

Remember to take the time to warm up thoroughly before beginning the exercises, and take time to cool down and stretch the muscles following each workout session.

These routines are an integral part of your training and will ensure that your muscles are supple and capable of performing the strenuous exercises required of them without risking injury.

Side Squats

Stand with your feet about two feet apart, with your toes pointing outward.

Hold a dumbbell in each hand, at hip height. Inhale as you slowly lower your body, until your thighs are parallel to the floor.

Hold the position and then tighten your buttocks and slowly come back to the starting position.

Repeat the exercise 10 times.

Muscles worked: Hamstrings, quadriceps, gluteus maximus/minimus

TOP TIP

◆ **Never allow your knees to go forward of your ankles**

Once mastered, this exercise may also be performed using a barbell lowered behind the shoulders, as shown below.

French Squats

This exercise may also be performed without the use of weights – without reducing the benefit.

Stand with feet a little more than shoulder width apart.

Take a disc weight and hold with both hands crossed in front of your chest.

Slowly inhale and lower your body, until your thighs are parallel to the floor.

Exhale as you tighten your buttocks, and return to the standing position.

Muscles worked: Quadriceps, gluteus maximus/minimus, hamstrings

TOP TIP

◆ **Keep your spine straight all the way through the movement**
◆ **Keep your feet flat on the floor**
◆ **Do not lean forward**

Once you have reached a certain level of general fitness, this exercise can also be performed in your local fitness club using the latest gym equipment, such as the Cybex Squat machine, opposite.

BODY TALK
Weight-bearing exercise and a healthy nutritious diet can help women to prevent osteoporosis that can come with the onset of menopause.

Forward Lunges

Stand with your back straight and feet shoulder width apart.

The movement may be performed holding a dumbbell in each hand, or with hands simply placed on hips.

Hold dumbbells at hip height with arms relaxed.

Breathe in, and with your right leg, take a comfortable step forward.

Keep the body straight and the foot in line with the hips.

Bend the right knee and lower the left knee towards the floor.

Stop when the lowered knee is about 10 inches (255mm) from the floor.

Breathe out as the right leg is drawn back and you return to the upright starting position.

Repeat with the left leg and then alternate legs until 10 repetitions have been achieved using each leg.

Muscles worked: *Quadriceps, hamstrings, gluteus maximus/minimus*

TOP TIPS
◆ **Keep hips square to the floor**
◆ **Keep the weight of your body centred over your hips**
◆ **Do not lock elbows**

BODY TALK
Allow 24 hours between exercise sessions to give your muscles time to rest and recover and your body time to refuel.

Step Ups

If you do not have a 'step' designed for this type of exercise, you can use either your stairs at home, or an object such as a strong heavy box (as long as it is stable and is able to take your weight without tipping over). A good working height would be 8 inches (approximately 200mm) or more, although you could begin with a lower step and gradually build up to a greater height as you become familiar with the exercise.

Be careful not to put unnecessary stress on your knees by raising the step too high. If you feel any discomfort following or during this exercise, reduce the height of the step.

Stand facing your step and step up with your left foot.

Then step up with your right foot, breathing out as you rise.

Now step down backwards with your left foot, and then with your right foot.

Repeat with your left leg leading, then continue to repeat the routine with alternating legs.

You can perform this exercise with or without dumbbells.

Muscles worked: *Hamstrings, adductors, quadriceps, gastrocnemius*

TOP TIPS
◆ **Remember to try to keep a good rhythm through the movement**
◆ **Always ensure that the whole of your foot is placed on to the step**
◆ **Keep your head up and straight – do not look down**
◆ **Listening to music can help you to keep your rhythm**
◆ **Take care to balance your weight squarely, without twisting the knee joints**

If you are using hand weights or dumbbells, choose simple arm exercises which are easily performed to the same rhythm as the step, taking care to keep the movement smooth to avoid putting a strain on joints and muscles.

Stair climbers, such as the Tectrix ClimbMax machine, right, offer excellent cardiovascular exercise combined with computerised training programs tailored to suit your own requirements.

Knee Lift to Rear

This exercise may also be performed using leg weights. For safety, it is recommended that you begin without weights and gradually introduce them, beginning with light weights and gradually increasing the weight as your level of fitness improves.

Take up a position on all fours – on your hands and knees.

Lift your right leg up behind you until the thigh is parallel to the floor.

Breathe in as you go through the movement.

Breathe out as you return to the starting position.

Repeat the exercise 10 times before beginning with the left leg.

Muscles worked: Hamstrings, gluteus maximus

TOP TIPS
◆ **Do not lift your thigh higher than parallel to the floor, as it can be stressful to the lower back**
◆ **Hold your stomach muscles in tight to help support your back**
◆ **Keep head and spine straight**

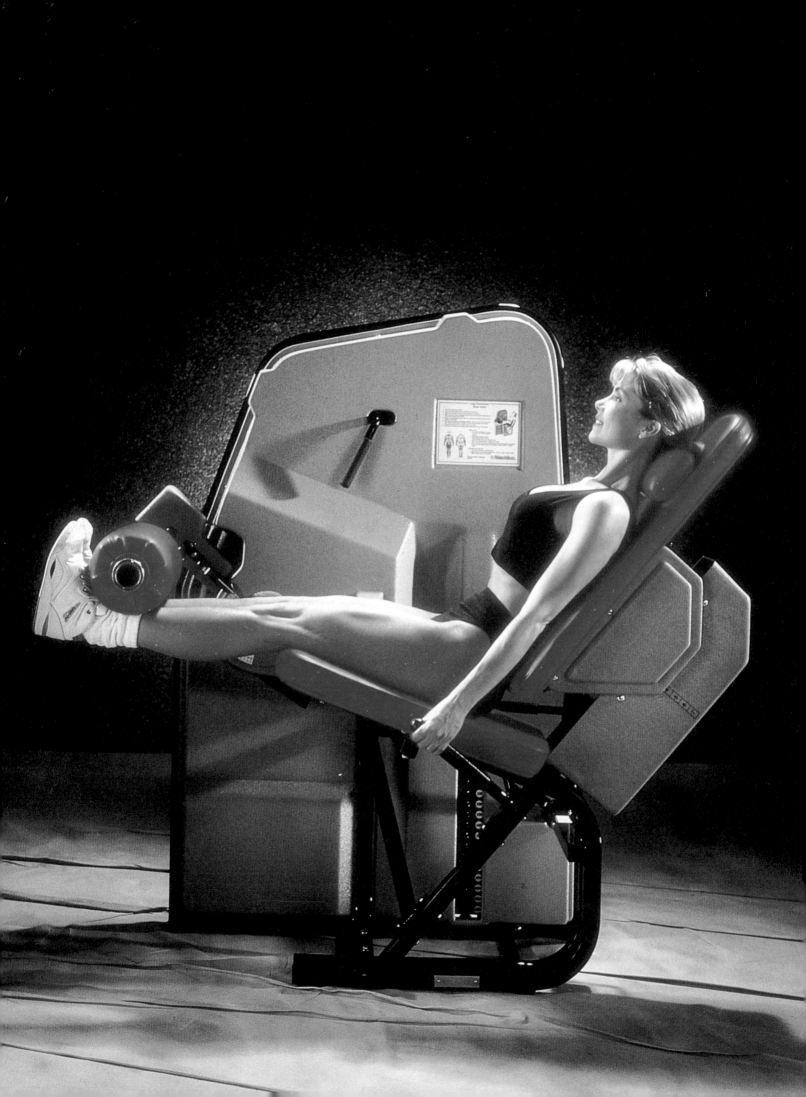

Inner and Outer Thigh Raises

Lie on your right side, with your back straight, hips square and feet together.

Support your head in your right hand and place your left hand in front of you for balance, as shown.

Ensure your right leg is straight, and bend your left leg at a right angle to your body for support.

Breathe out as you slowly raise your right leg as high as possible.

Hold briefly and breathe in as you lower your leg.

Repeat 10 times using each leg.

Muscles worked: *Hamstrings, adductors, quadriceps*

To develop this exercise and further strengthen your legs, begin the exercise as before, but rest the bent leg on the straight leg to increase the weight lifted. See below.

Another exercise to strengthen the thighs can be seen below. Stand with feet four feet apart with hands on hips. Bend knees to a squat position, hold, and repeat 10 times.

The Nautilus Leg Extension machine, pictured left, provides excellent strengthening exercise for the legs.

Leg Curl

Wearing leg weights, stand with feet together, and place your hands on the back of a chair for support.

Bend one knee until the lower leg is parallel to the floor.

Keep thighs straight, do not move upper leg.

Slowly lower your foot to the floor, inhaling through the movement, and then slowly exhale and bring your foot back up until the lower leg is once again parallel to the floor.

Repeat 10 times for each leg.

Muscles worked: Hamstrings, Quadriceps, adductors, soleus

TOP TIPS

◆ **Keep your buttocks tight to assist your lower back**
◆ **Always make sure that your leg weights are fitted correctly and are not too heavy for your level of fitness**

This exercise may also be performed at your fitness club using a machine. See Cybex Seated Leg Curl machine, right.

HOW ENERGY IS PRODUCED
Food is consumed and taken into the body where digestion takes place.
Glucose is produced and absorbed into the bloodstream where it enters the muscles, combines with oxygen and is broken down into energy, producing waste products in the form of carbon dioxide and water.

BODY TALK
When glucose burns, it combines with oxygen in a reaction called respiration. The energy exchanged in this process creates heat which makes the body hot.

Dead Lifts

This is a very good exercise for developing the lower back, but can cause injury to lower back, buttocks and thighs if too much weight is lifted too soon. Always begin with light weights, and remember to stop immediately if you feel any discomfort. This exercise can be performed using dumbbells or a barbell.

Stand with your feet shoulder width apart.

Bend down until your thighs are parallel with the floor, hold the barbell or dumbbells just above your feet, with arms on the outside of your legs.

Keeping your back straight and your chin up, look straight ahead.

Breathe out as you slowly lift the weights up from the floor, until you are standing straight.

Breathe in as you slowly lower the weights back to the floor and resume the starting position.

Repeat the exercise 10 times

Muscles worked: *Quadriceps, gluteus maximus/minimus, hamstrings*

TOP TIPS

◆ Keep your head up and look straight ahead

◆ Keep your feet firmly placed with knees apart

◆ Keep your arms straight without locking the elbows

◆ This exercise can also be performed in a fitness club where the equipment allows you to lift a much greater weight

HOW THE BODY WORKS DURING EXERCISE

When muscles work hard during exercise they use up the oxygen in the blood which is then replaced with carbon dioxide. They also generate heat which creates a reaction telling the skin to sweat, which cools the body as it evaporates from the surface of the skin.

The heart beats faster, increasing blood circulation as more blood is sent away from the muscles to the surface of the skin to be cooled.

More oxygen is taken into the lungs as the breathing rate increases and more carbon dioxide is expelled as waste.

These reactions continue after exercise until all the body's processes are stabilised and functioning normally.

Bent Over Rowing

Use a strong chair, bench, or other suitable sturdy object.

Lean on the edge of the chair with your right hand.

Take a dumbbell in your left hand ensuring that your arm is extended straight down towards the floor.

Keep your shoulders square to the floor and pull the dumbbell straight up towards your chest.

Keep your arm close to your body at all times, and remember to breathe out as you lift.

Slowly lower the dumbbell to the starting position as you breathe in.

Repeat the exercise 10 times using each arm

This exercise may also be performed using a barbell, but care must be taken to perform the exercise in a controlled and balanced manner, to avoid putting stress on the back.

Muscles worked: *Latissimus dorsi, biceps*

TOP TIPS
◆ **Do not arch your back**
◆ **Keep your stomach tucked in**

Rowing machines such as the Cybex Seated Row machine, right, provide excellent all round cardiovascular exercise, working back, arm, shoulder and leg muscles.

Upright Rowing

Stand with your feet shoulder width apart and hips tucked in.

Hold a dumbbell in each hand, or a barbell in front of your thighs with palms facing towards you.

Pull the weights up along the front of your body until at shoulder height, lifting your elbows out as you breathe out.

Slowly lower the weights to the starting position, remembering to breathe in as you lower.

Repeat the exercise 10 times.

Muscles worked: Biceps, triceps, pectoral, trapezius, anterior deltoids

TOP TIPS

◆ **Do not allow your hips to come forward**

◆ **Keep your elbows high and your wrists straight**

◆ **When using dumbbells, they should always remain parallel to the floor**

◆ **Keep your head up and look straight ahead**

THE HEART OF THE MATTER
*The human heart beats approximately 70 times per minute.
It is unique in that it is the only muscle of the body which never tires.
During an average lifespan of 70 years it beats about 2,500 million times and pumps 60 million gallons (227 million litres) of blood around the body.
The heart weighs less than 1lb (0.45 kg) and is about the size of a fist.*

FITNESS FACT
*Adrenaline is a hormone which prepares the body for fast emergency action – the fight or flight reaction common to humans and animals.
It increases the speed of all body processes and enables the body to run for its' life.
Adrenaline is triggered by the excitement of competition and exercise and primes the body for action.*

Box Press Up

Kneel down on the floor, place a towel under your knees for padding if you wish, or use an exercise mat.

Lean forward and place your hands beside your chest and bend the knees

You may raise your calves off the floor and cross your ankles.

Keeping your knees on the floor, breathe out as you push your body up until your arms are straight.

Hold, then slowly lower, breathing in as you return to the starting position.

Repeat 10 times, or as many times as you are able to do without pausing.

Muscles worked: *Pectorals, triceps, anterior deltoids*

TOP TIPS
◆ **Keep your upper body straight**
◆ **Do not lock the elbows**
◆ **Do not crane your neck forward as you press your chest down to the floor**
◆ **Work in a controlled, steady rhythm**
◆ **Keep your elbows close to your side**
◆ **Use press up handles for added height**

Press ups may also be performed using press up handles which raise your upper body further from the floor.

Chest press machines also work the chest areas, see page 85.

Press Up

Lie face down on the floor.

Place your hands by your chest with legs straight out behind and feet together – balls of your feet fixed onto the floor.

Press your body up until your arms are straight, remembering to breathe out as you press up.

Slowly lower your body back to the starting position breathing in as you lower.

Try to do the exercise in a continuous rhythmic movement, as many times as you can.

Muscles worked: Pectorals, triceps, anterior deltoids

As you become more advanced, you can extend the press up by supporting your feet on a bench or a step.

TOP TIP
◆ **Do not hollow your back as you press up – keep it flat**
◆ **Do not lock the elbows**
◆ **Remember to breathe correctly**

If you wish to work a larger area of your chest, back and arms, you can place your arms wider apart, at about 12 inches (30cm) either side of your head as shown below.

Standard Press Up   Advanced Press Up

Flys

Lie on your back on a bench.

Place your feet firmly on the floor as shown, or bring your knees up and place your feet on the bench.

Take a dumbbell in each hand and hold it directly above your chest, palms facing each other and the dumbbells touching.

Ensure that your elbows are slightly bent and slowly open your arms until your arms are parallel to the floor.

Breathe out as you lower. Breathe in as you bring the dumbbells back to the starting position.

Repeat the exercise 10 times

This exercise may also be performed without a bench, lying on the floor using an exercise mat or a thick towel to lie on.

Muscles worked: *Pectorals, anterior deltoids*

TOP TIP

◆ **When lying on your back and lifting heavy weights, it is advisable to perform the exercise with the help of a partner who can assist and ensure your safety.**

Shoulder Press

Sit on a firm chair or use a bench.

Take a dumbbell in each hand, bend the elbows and hold the weights at shoulder height, close to your body, with palms facing forwards.

Breathe out as you press the dumbbells straight up to arms length, then breathe in as you lower to the starting position.

Repeat the exercise 10 times.

Muscles worked: Anterior deltoids, deltoids, trapezius, triceps

TOP TIPS

◆ **Keep your back straight**
◆ **Do not try to lift too heavier dumbbells or a barbell until you are lifting lighter weights with ease, as this could be dangerous**
◆ **Perform the exercise with a steady, controlled rhythm**
◆ **Keep your feet flat on the floor**

This exercise may also be performed using a barbell. Begin holding the bar in front of your chest at shoulder height. Slowly raise, then carefully lower behind your head, keeping the bar level.

Once you are familiar with the exercise, you may wish to use the shoulder press machine at your local fitness club, enabling you to perform the same movements using the same muscles.

Resistance machines allow safe use of heavier weights under controlled conditions, with the assistance of qualified staff who can offer valuable advice to help you with your training.

Dumbbell Press

Lie on your back on a bench.

Place your feet firmly on the floor or bring your knees up and place your feet on the bench.

Take a dumbbell in each hand, palms facing inward, with your elbows extended out to the side at 90 degrees, directly above your shoulders.

Press the dumbbells up and towards each other in front of you, breathing out as you lift.

Hold, then slowly lower the weights back to the starting position, breathing in as you lower.

Repeat the exercise 10 times.

This exercise may also be performed without a bench, lying on the floor using an exercise mat or a thick towel to lie on.

Muscles worked: *Anterior deltoids, deltoids, trapezius, triceps*

A barbell may be used instead of dumbbells. For safety, it is wise to ask a friend to assist when lifting a bar with heavy weights whilst lying on your back.

FITNESS FACTS
Always train the largest muscle groups first (chest, arms and legs) when energy levels are high.

◆

Extended workouts can sap the desire and enthusiasm to train and slow down progress. Make your training sessions interesting and vary your program with cross training.

◆

Complete your workout at set times — before work, lunchtimes or after work, and allow yourself time for other responsibilities and activities.

◆

Cramp occurs when muscles contract abnormally, cutting off the blood supply. It is commonly caused by an imbalance of body salts, particularly calcium, which is lost via perspiration through the skin.

Side Lateral Raise

Sit on a firm chair or use a bench.

Hold a dumbbell in each hand with palms facing your sides, and arms relaxed and straight.

With your arms straight but your elbows not fixed, raise both dumbbells straight up to the side, until they reach shoulder height.

Breathe out as you raise your arms, hold, then slowly lower to the starting position, breathing in as you return to the starting position.

Repeat the exercise 10 times.

Muscles worked: Deltoids

TOP TIPS
◆ **Keep your back straight**
◆ **Do not bend your wrists**
◆ **Keep your feet flat on the floor**

This exercise may also be performed – standing, or seated – with feet firmly on the floor and the upper body bent forwards, parallel to the floor.

Keep your feet together.

Raise the dumbbell slowly out to the sides until your arms are parallel to the floor and raised to your shoulders.

Hold briefly and return to the starting position, controlling the movement.

Muscles worked: Posterior deltoids

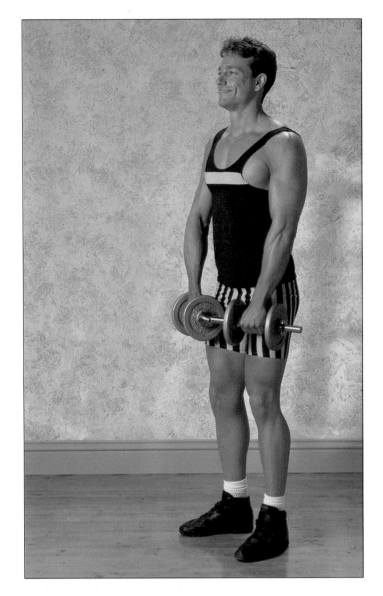

Front Shoulder Lifts

Stand with feet shoulder width apart and back straight.

Hold a dumbbell in each hand with palms facing towards the front of your body.

Start by raising your right arm up into the air in front of your body, until the weight is at shoulder height.

Hold.

Breathe out as you raise your arm, then slowly lower, breathing in as you return to the starting position.

Raise your left arm and repeat the exercise 10 times with each arm.

Muscles worked: *Anterior deltoids, pectorals*

TOP TIPS

◆ **Do not arch your back**

◆ **Use a mirror to ensure that the movements are straight and controlled**

◆ **Keep knees slightly bent**

FITNESS FACTS

Fitness may be measured by how quickly the heart recovers to its normal rate following vigorous exercise. An average healthy adult's heart beats about 65 to 70 times per minute.

◆

An athlete's heart rate which may reach up to 180 beats per minute during extreme strenuous exercise, should return to normal after 2 or 3 minutes. The heart of an unfit adult could take as long as 10 minutes to return to normal following exercise.

◆

Muscles, tendons and skin contain pain receptors which warn of injury. It is wise to stop exercising as soon as pain indicates the possibility of a strained muscle, sprained joint or a torn tendon, rather than continue and risk a more serious or even permanent injury.

◆

Minor aches and pains following strenuous exercise may be alleviated by a relaxing soak in a comfortable warm bath. Add aromatic oils, seaweed or herbal preparations to ease those tired muscles.

Bicep Curls

Stand with feet shoulder width apart, hips tucked in and shoulders dropped and relaxed.

Hold a dumbbell in each hand in front of your body, with palms facing forward, resting against your thighs.

Bending from the elbow only, bring the dumbbell in your right hand up until it touches the front of your chest.

Breathe out as you raise the dumbbell towards you, then slowly breathe in as you return to the starting position.

Repeat the exercise 10 times with each arm.

This exercise may also be performed using a barbell which will work both arms at the same time.

Muscles worked: Biceps, brachialis

Kickbacks

Use a strong chair or a bench for balance.

Lean forward and rest your left hand on the back of the chair.

Hold a dumbbell in the right hand.

Keep your back straight and lift the upper arm until it is parallel to the floor, keeping the lower arm vertical.

Press the dumbbell back until the entire arm is parallel to the floor, breathing out as you lift the weight.

Hold for a few seconds, then slowly lower as you breathe in.

Repeat the exercise 10 times using each arm.

Muscles worked: Biceps, triceps, latissimus dorsi

TOP TIPS

◆ **Move slowly and feel your muscles work**

◆ **Do not swing the dumbbell**

◆ **Keep the lifting arm close to your body in a controlled movement**

TOP TIPS

◆ **Do not swing the dumbbell – control the movement**

◆ **Keep the elbow close to your body**

◆ **Working with your back pressed against a wall will help to keep the back straight**

FITNESS FACTS
Do not suddenly expose your warm muscles to cool or cold temperatures immediately after exercise, cool down slowly to prevent sudden stiffness or tension.

Overhead Extension

Sit on a chair or use a bench.

Keeping your back straight.

Hold a single dumbbell in both hands behind your head, with palms up.

Keep upper arms close to your head.

Bend your arms at the elbow, breathing in as you slowly lower the dumbbell behind your neck as far as you can.

Hold, then breathe out as you straighten your arms above your head, then lower and repeat the exercise 10 times for each arm.

Muscles worked: *Triceps*

This exercise may be performed at your local fitness club or gym using a machine such as the Cybex Overhead Extension/Pullover, right.

TOP TIPS

◆ Keep your head straight, looking straight ahead with chin up

◆ Do not arch your back

BODY TALK

The human body is more complex than any machine or computer.

◆

The average person breathes in and out 16 times per minute at rest. Each breath exchanges about 30 cubic inches (500ml) of fresh and used air.

◆

The human body is made up of more than 10 million million cells.

◆

Oxygen is needed by the cells of the body to help change food into chemical energy. Without oxygen a cell will die in four minutes.

◆

The normal human body temperature is about 98.4 degrees F (37 degrees C).

Dips

Use a bench, a sturdy chair, or the bottom of the stairs.

Sit on the bench and grasp the seat each side.

Supporting your weight on the heels of your hands, push your body away from the chair and lean out with legs straight, so that you are resting on your heels and taking your weight on your hands.

Slowly bend your elbows until your upper arms are parallel to the floor.

Breathe out as you lower, hold, and then push yourself back up to the starting position.

Breathe in as you return.

Repeat the exercise 10 times.

Muscles worked: *Triceps*

TOP TIPS
◆ **Keep your back straight**
◆ **Perform the exercise with a slow, steady movement to balance and control your weight**

Dips may also be performed without the use of a bench, see below. Sit on the floor, lean back, with hands placed on the floor behind your body.

With weight supported by hands and heels, gently dip the body by bending the elbows.

BODY TALK
The human body contains about 60,000 miles (96,500km) of blood vessels – enough to go twice around the earth.
◆
The human body contains enough fat to make seven cakes of soap.
◆
The human body contains enough iron to make a one inch (25mm) nail.
◆
The human liver can weigh as much as 4lb (1.8kg) and at rest contains up to 25% of the body's blood.

Leg Extensions

Lie on your back on a bench, or use an exercise mat or a towel on the floor if you find this more comfortable.

Link your hands behind your head, or grasp the rungs on the bench.

Cross your ankles, and bring your knees up to your chest, or as close to your body as you can.

Extend your legs out straight, keeping them 20 inches (50cm) off the floor, with knees together.

Breathe out as you straighten.

Hold, then return to the starting position, breathing in as you return.

Repeat the exercise as many times as you can.

Each leg may also be worked separately, with, or without leg weights, see below.

Leg extensions will work the lower part of the stomach.

Muscles worked: External obliques, quadriceps, hamstrings

TOP TIPS

◆ **Place a towel under your back for support**
◆ **The higher you raise your legs the easier the exercise becomes**

You can use a Leg Extension machine at your local fitness club. See page 48.

Side Bends

Stand with feet shoulder width apart.

Hold a dumbbell in your left hand, and place your right hand behind your head. See picture on right.

Keep the left arm straight.

Bend to the side as far as you can.

Breathe in as you bend to the side, hold, then return to the starting position, breathing out until the body is straight.

Repeat the exercise at least 10 times on each side.

This exercise may also be performed holding a dumbbell in each hand, as shown above.

Muscles worked: *External obliques*

TOP TIPS

◆ **Keep your neck straight at all times**

◆ **Do not put any force behind your neck to assist the movement**

Crunch Sit Ups

Lie on your back with your knees bent and feet flat on the floor, hips width apart.

Place your hands beside your head with finger tips just touching.

Press your back firmly on the floor.

Breathe out as you slowly raise your head and shoulders off the floor.

Hold, then lower.

Crunch Sit Ups work the upper and middle areas of the stomach muscles.

Muscles worked: *External obliques*

TOP TIPS

◆ **Keep your head in line with your spine**

◆ **Keep your abdominal muscles tight**

◆ **Only brush the floor with your shoulders before rising again**

◆ **Use your elbows as a balance, but do not pull on your neck or the back of your head to assist your return to the starting position**

Twisted Sit Ups

Lie on your back with your knees bent and feet flat on the floor.

Place your hands behind your head and press your elbows back.

Cross your right foot over and rest it on your left knee. Breathe in.

Breathe out as you slowly raise your left shoulder upwards and across your body towards your right knee.

Hold briefly, then breathe in as you slowly lower to the starting position.

Repeat the movement 10 times each side.

TOP TIP

◆ **Work both sides equally**

Reverse Curls

This exercise may be performed on the floor or using a bench.

Lie flat on your back with your arms by your sides, palms on the floor or exercise mat.

If you are using a bench, bring your hands over your head and grip the edge of the bench to give you support.

Begin with legs together and straight.

Raise legs slowly until they are at 90 degrees to your body, vertical to the floor, or, if you can, bring the feet further over your body until your feet are above your head.

Hold, then lower, repeating the movement 10 times.

There are many variations of the abdominal crunch and sit up, above. The abdominal training machine also works the same stomach muscles. See page 21.

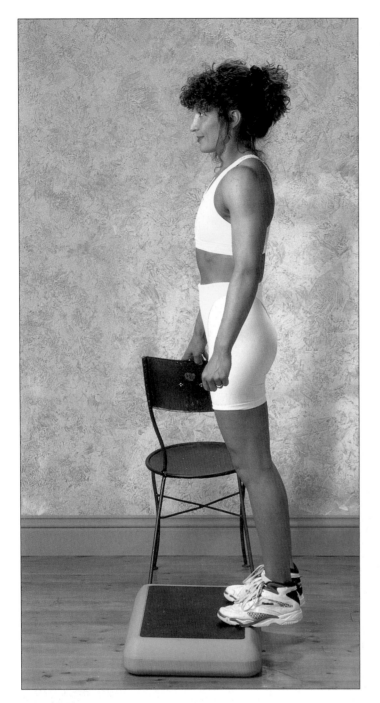
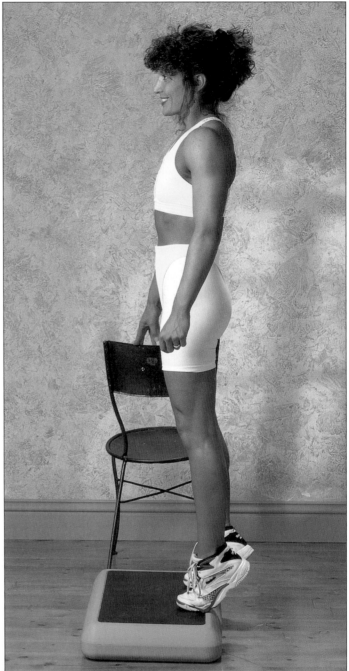

Standing Calf Raises

Use a step, the bottom of the stairs or a suitable sturdy object which will safely support your weight.

Stand with the balls of your feet on the edge of the step.

Extend one arm and use the back of a chair for balance.

Rise up on the balls of your feet, breathing out as you go through the movement.

Slowly lower your heels down as far as you can, breathing in as you lower.

You may perform this exercise holding a dumbbell in one hand, or two dumbbells if your balance is good and you do not risk sudden movements which may be harmful.

Repeat the exercise 10 times.

Muscles worked: *Gastrocnemius*

TOP TIPS

◆ **Maintain a slow and controlled movement**

◆ **Keep your hips straight and your body square**

BODY TALK

The inner ear enables the body to balance. A maze of passages and fluid filled canals are sensitive to currents created by movements of the head. The brain senses the body's position in relation to gravity and movement, and with the aid of sensors in the muscles and messages received from the eyes, monitors posture and enables the body to adjust to maintain balance.

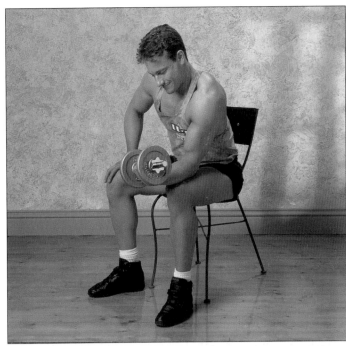

Wrist Curls

Sit on a chair, leaning forward with your forearms on your thighs.

Hold a dumbbell, with wrist on top of your knee and palms facing up.

Roll the wrist up as high as you can, breathing out, then slowly lower the dumbbell back to the starting position as you breathe in.

Repeat the exercise 10 times

Muscles worked: Brachioradialis, biceps

TOP TIPS

◆ Begin using light weights and gradually work up to heavier weights or increase repetitions

◆ As you lower the dumbbell back down, rest the back of your fists on your knees

You may use two dumbbells at the same time, or use a barbell, to work both wrists together.

Developing a Training Program

Once you have become familiar with the warm up exercises and mastered the techniques for the weight training exercises, you will wish to work out using a program of exercises designed specifically with your own objectives and level of fitness in mind.

A training program will assist with your fitness training at all levels – whether your aim is purely to achieve general fitness and improve body tone, to increase fitness for a specific sporting activity, or if your objective is to work on specific areas of the body and approach training with weights with body building in mind – perhaps even competition.

It is important not to significantly increase your exercise program too soon and overstress your muscles. A varied program of exercises for beginners will involve lifting light weights for a determined number of repetitions per exercise for a few weeks.

The right program for you

Establish a program that suits you, using weights you can lift without difficulty. It is not necessary to lift heavier weights until your program becomes easy and you feel the need to progress to a more demanding program using heavier weights. Increase your weights gradually, 2 – 5lbs (approximately 1 – 2.25 kilograms) at a time.

TOP TIP
◆ When the exercises become too easy, you will know it is time to increase the weights

Use light weights if your aim is to shape up and achieve body tone and general fitness. Increase the number of repetitions performed if you wish to progress your training program.

Gradually continue to use heavier weights if you wish to increase muscle mass, without increasing the number of repetitions per exercise.

To ensure the maximum benefit and to avoid unnecessary stress or risk of injury, continue to workout using your training program three or four times per week for approximately 6-8 weeks before progressing to a more advanced and demanding program.

Consistency and dedication will produce results and you will soon notice improvements in your shape, stamina and general sense of well-being.

Monitor Improvements

If certain areas appear slow to improve, you will know to adjust the next level of program to add particular exercises or increase the weights, to concentrate on those particular muscle groups.

All the weight training exercises in this book can be performed using light weight hand dumbbells, heavy dumbbells or even a barbell where required. It is important to choose the weights with which you are comfortable.

Your program should begin with exercises for the larger muscle groups, when your energy level is at its highest, working down to the smaller muscle groups, where less energy is required. The order should be:

1. Chest, back, thighs
2. Shoulders, biceps, triceps
3. Calves and forearms.

It is important to perform floor exercises to stretch and strengthen legs, buttocks and the three areas of abdominal muscles at each workout.

When designing your training program, be sure to achieve a balance of exercises to work the entire body. Imbalance caused by concentrating on one area of the body will not only risk injury to overstressed muscles, but may damage opposing muscle groups which have to compensate for the stress, and may even cause damage to the joints.

If it is your intention to concentrate on developing certain muscle groups, your program should also include exercises to strengthen the opposing muscle groups as each group requires the assistance of another to work.

Emphasis on developing the biceps whilst neglecting the triceps, for example, may result in an injury to the triceps. A well proportioned fit body is more attractive and far healthier than a body which is well developed in some areas and neglected in others.

It is wise to weight train only every other day. As a beginner, you may wish to train on Mondays and Wednesdays

Exercise Program for Beginners

	EXERCISE	SETS	REPS	✔
MONDAY	Barbell Press	2	10	
	Upright Row	2	10	
	Dumbbell Flys	2	10	
	Sit Ups	2	20	
	Squats	2	10	
	Calf Raises	2	10	
WEDNESDAY	Dumbbell Press	2	10	
	Bent Over Rowing	2	10	
	Sit Ups	2	20	
	Lateral Raises	2	10	
	Upright Rowing	2	10	
	Tricep Extensions	2	10	
FRIDAY	Upright Rowing	2	10	
	Dumbbell Flys	2	10	
	Squats	2	10	
	Sit Ups	2	20	
	Bicep Curls	2	10	
	Leg Curls	2	10	

Aerobic exercises for cross-training:

TUESDAY: *Swimming*

THURSDAY: *Aerobics Class*

PLUS — Family Cycling at Weekend

and participate in other aerobic activities such as swimming or cycling on Tuesdays and Thursdays (see cross training, page 88). The program chart above shows a few examples of exercises featured in this book, but it is important that you create a program which is specifically designed to suit you.

The exercise program above features six basic movements for each of three training sessions, as examples. Ten or more repetitions (reps) are performed in two separate sets for each exercise. Continue with the same program for six weeks before increasing the weights lifted or the number of repetitions or sets performed. Do not weight train two days running.

Exercise Program

WEEK No.............　DATE BEGINNING.................................

	EXERCISES	SETS	REPS	✔
MONDAY (or TUESDAY)				
WEDNESDAY (or THURSDAY)				
FRIDAY (or SATURDAY)				

Aerobic exercises for cross-training:

TUESDAY:
(or WEDNESDAY)

THURSDAY:
(or FRIDAY)

Set Yourself Goals

When beginning a new exercise program it is wise to set yourself goals. Here are eight steps to help you train to achieve your aims:

◆ Always be realistic. Remember that if you are realistic you will be able to reach your goals and it will encourage you to continue to achieve greater goals and objectives.

◆ Focus, and ensure that you make time to workout. Keep to the time allocated without being distracted.

◆ Record your workouts in a note book, read your notes at the end of the last workout in the program and try to improve and develop the next program.

◆ Be specific about your objectives and why you are training. Plan to achieve the goals you want.

◆ Set yourself goals to aim for (holiday, birthday etc).

◆ Decide what you want from your training – to become fitter, to gain muscle, or to become generally more healthy and more alert.

◆ It is preferable to work out with your training partner, wife, girl friend, or friend – don't make excuses not to train, but don't become a training bore.

◆ Reward yourself when you reach your goals or targets, in order to set yourself higher targets next time.

◆ Rest after each set of exercises for between 1-3 minutes, allowing your body to recover sufficiently to enable you to complete the next set without pausing for breath.

Copy this chart and use it to create your own weekly training program. You may choose to weight train Mondays, Wednesdays and Fridays, and cross train on Tuesdays and Thursdays. Alternatively, you may wish to weight train Tuesdays, Thursdays and Saturdays and cross train on Wednesdays and Fridays. Don't be a training bore – involve your family and friends in your cross training and choose activities which everyone can enjoy.

1. A training program for general fitness

Include one exercise for each area of the body.

Use light weights and perform 10 repetitions (1 set) of each exercise.

Maintain your level of heart rate during the exercises by not resting for too long between sets.

Once the program becomes easy, perform 2 sets of each exercise.

This program should be performed once or twice per week.

Aerobic exercise such as swimming, cycling, jogging or aerobics classes should also be included to achieve overall fitness.

A general fitness program will not alter your body shape or increase muscle mass.

Combined with a sensible healthy diet it will assist in weight loss and contribute to a sense of increased energy and general well-being.

2. A training program for toning and strengthening the muscles

Using light weights, include one exercise for each part of the body.

Increase the repetitions to 12-15 per set and perform 3 or 4 sets per exercise.

Rest briefly between sets.

This type of program, performed 1 – 3 times per week will achieve overall body toning and fitness without noticeably altering the shape of the body.

Aerobic exercises should also be included in this program.

3. A training program to shape and strengthen the body

Based on the program 2 for toning and strengthening, this program will include 3 or 4 workouts per week lasting between 45 – 90 minutes per session, using gradually increasing weights and 3 or 4 sets of 8 – 12 repetitions.

All areas of the body should be worked during the week and care should be taken to warm up correctly before the workout and stretch and cool down at the end.

Additional aerobic exercise will add variety to your program and ensure overall fitness.

4. A training program to increase muscle mass (body building)

Based on program 3 for strength and shape, perform fewer repetitions (4-8) using heavier weights.

The ideal weight for these exercises will be the heaviest you can use but still achieve the final repetition in any set.

At least 4 workouts per week lasting 90 minutes per session will be required if your aim is to add substantial muscle mass and alter the shape of your body.

5. A training program following injury

Following advice from your doctor, you may return to your training program taking care not to over-stress the injured muscles or put undue stress on opposing muscle groups.

Warm up well first.

Exercise the injured area first. Increase the demands you put on the area very gradually, and take care to use lighter weights until the injured area has recovered sufficiently to cope with the stress.

Work the injured area more often for shorter periods before returning to your usual training program.

TOP TIP

The results of any training program will be quicker and more dramatic depending on the frequency and length of each training session

6. A training program to increase and maintain fitness for a specific sport

Weight training will improve specific muscle groups used in particular sports.

Exercises to improve and strengthen certain muscle groups may be added to a general program designed to improve overall fitness and general body strength.

Be sure to exercise opposing muscle groups evenly to achieve balance and avoid the risk of injury.

Using a Fitness Club or Gym

The latest equipment and helpful advice available at your local fitness club will be invaluable to your overall training program. Your family will enjoy using the facilities too.

Once you feel you wish to progress your training and use the equipment available at a fitness club or gym, you will wish to choose a suitable club, and this may be a difficult decision to make. You may choose a fitness club, or a gymnasium, depending on the facilities available and your own training requirements, but how do you begin to select the club ideally suited to your needs?

What facilities should the fitness club offer?

You will need the use of a fully equipped fitness gym, and an indoor swimming pool would provide a valuable opportunity for swimming to be incorporated as cross-training into your fitness program.

Many clubs may ask prospective members to complete a simple health screening questionnaire to establish any medical conditions and family health history, in order to ensure that the individual is not at risk.

You may then be asked to undertake a thorough fitness assessment to determine your level of health and fitness before a suitable program of exercise is planned. This involves tests to establish your resting heart rate and a cycle test to indicate current fitness.

You may also be asked to take a body fat test. This is simple and painless – estimating body fat percentage using callipers applied to certain places of the body where the skin is pinched.

Does the club provide supervision in the gym at all times by qualified instructors?

You will be shown how to use the equipment and may need a little advice and assistance from the staff if you are to advance your training without risking injury. Many clubs offer to help you create a suitable fitness program designed specifically for you, and will monitor you with professional fitness testing. This may be of particular benefit to your personal training program.

Will you find it easy to approach the staff for advice and assistance?

When you viewed the club, were the staff friendly and welcoming? Did they offer to show you around the club and explain the facilities?

What is the cost of joining a club?

The cost of becoming a member of a private fitness club may vary according to the controlled level of membership. A club with fewer members is likely to cost more to join than a club with a higher number of members.

A choice of different membership packages may be available – peak membership will allow you to use the facilities at any time. Day-time, or off-peak membership is less expensive but limited to quieter times of the day which may, or may not suit you.

The facilities available to members without additional cost will be clearly indicated, but facilities such as sun-beds are often charged extra. New members may also pay an initial joining fee.

The advantage of joining a private club is that you may choose to pay monthly, direct from your bank, to spread the cost of membership.

How easy will it be to join the club of your choice?

There may be a waiting list to join the club of your choice, in which case you may choose to continue your training at home until you can join as a member, or look for another suitable club.

Many clubs insist that new members undertake a fitness assessment before using the equipment unsupervised, and you may agree that this a wise precaution, indicating a sensible and safety conscious approach to the management of the facilities and care and consideration towards members.

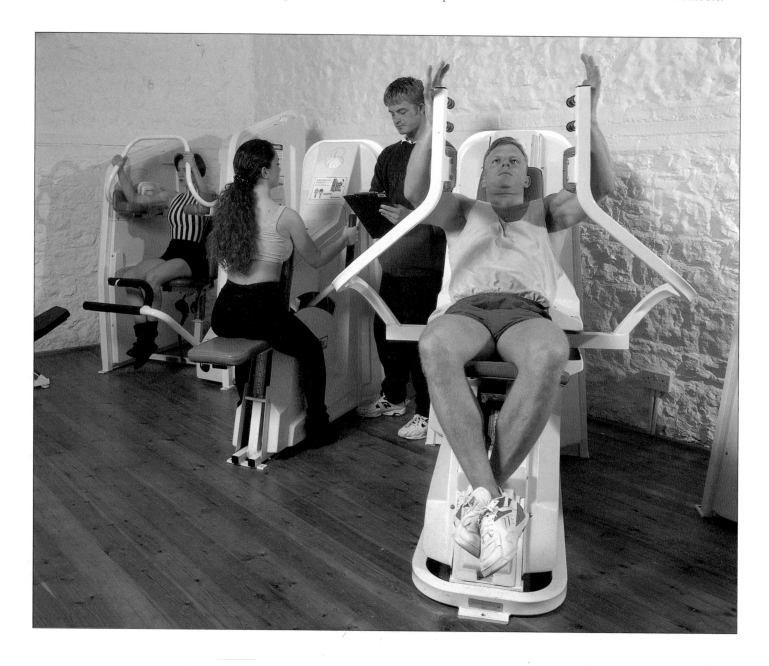

Do you wish to take advantage of other cross training opportunities?

Many clubs offer group classes for aerobics, step-aerobics, circuit training (exercises using various equipment to work specific muscle groups), boxercise (circuit training combined with boxing training), aquacise (aerobic exercise in water), dance and many other group activities. You may wish to join a suitable class as part of your cross training to increase your general fitness and aerobic capacity.

Additional facilities available to members may include squash courts, sauna, steam-room, solarium, spa bath, massage, physiotherapy, sports injury clinic, health and beauty salon and aromatherapy. If these facilities are of use to you, it will be worth joining a club where you may take full advantage of such a wide range of additional facilities and activities.

Many clubs have catering facilities and bars, offering the opportunity for social gatherings. It is vital to ensure fluid and carbohydrate replenishment following a strenuous workout, but remember that alcohol should be avoided following exercise.

Is the club conveniently located?

If you can walk, jog or cycle to the gym as part of your warm up you will save time warming up once you arrive. If you have to drive to the club, is it easy to park your car, and is the car park lit at night for safety?

If the club is within walking or jogging distance to your place of work, you may be able to schedule your training sessions to fit in with your lunch-breaks, or on your way home from work, using the time travelling as part of your warm up.

The Nautilus Abdominal machine works the stomach muscles. See exercises pages 69-73.

Does the club have a good atmosphere?

A well-equipped, pleasant, clean and well ventilated place to train will make a difference to the enjoyment you gain from your exercise program. Does the club play music which encourages a vigorous workout? Are the changing rooms, lockers and showers good?

Do the staff appear happy and interested in their work, and do other club members make you feel welcome? If the answer to all these questions is YES – then this could be the ideal club for you!

A fitness assessment will enable you to develop a suitable personal training program.

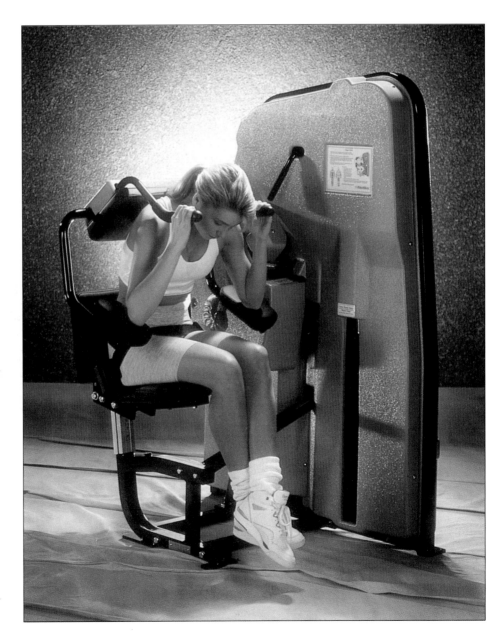

Exercises Using the Latest Equipment in a Fitness Club or Gym

The following exercises are examples of advanced exercises based on those you have performed at home. Once you reach a certain level of fitness and confidence, you will be able to progress to similar, more strenuous exercises using the equipment available in a gym or health club.

With professional assistance and advice at your private fitness club or gym, the exercise equipment is specially designed to allow you to lift heavier weights and to assist you to work your body generally. You may then decide to concentrate on developing certain muscle groups, if desired.

Right: The Keiser Seated Chest Press machine works the same muscles as the chest and shoulder exercises you would perform at home using free weights.

Below: One of the latest pieces of equipment to be found in the gym is the Nautilus TIME MACHINE – a multi-station machine featuring five different movements.

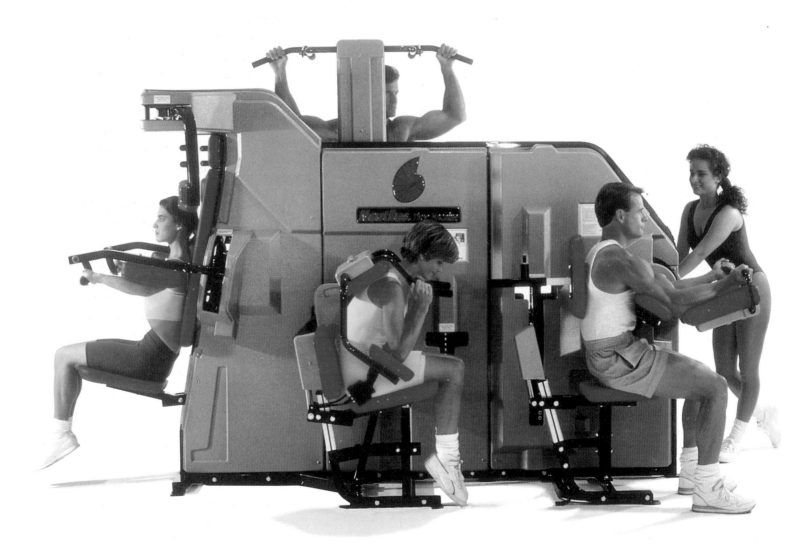

Peck Deck

This machine is very good for developing the chest and uses the same movement as Flys (see page 60) which can be performed at home as a floor exercise or using a bench. The machine controls the movement to ensure that you are only working the chest muscles.

Leg Curl Machine

This machine works the hamstrings (the backs of your upper legs), and the angle of the machine ensures that there is no strain placed upon any other area of the body. This exercise may be performed at home using leg weights, see page 50.

Bench Press

This machine works the shoulders and inner back. The machine stipulates the sequence of movements, and ensures that you only train the area specifically required. This exercise may be performed at home using free weights, see pages 61-62.

TOP TIPS

◆ As you train, fluids will be lost through sweating, and it is extremely important to drink water, even during your training, in order to compensate for the loss of water while you are exercising

◆ Never eat less than one hour before training, as this is bad for digestion and you will soon tire

◆ Lively music can help to achieve a much more harmonious training experience

◆ Training is much more enjoyable in the company of friends

◆ If you do not understand an exercise or a piece of equipment, it is important that you always ask the instructor to explain fully for reasons of safety

◆ Breathing is an essential part of training. Assume that you breathe out during the press or pull movement, and breathe in as you return the weight to the starting position. Never hold your breath during an exercise, as this can deprive the body of the necessary oxygen and raise the blood pressure

◆ You should always wear a weight training belt when training with free-standing and heavy weights

◆ When training with a partner, it will help you both if you count out each others repetitions in each set. This will encourage you both to finish each set of exercises

◆ If you are working the back of your legs, ankles, calves, and find that you are straining the back of your legs, then place a strong book under your heels

◆ Keep your back straight when performing exercises, unless otherwise instructed – always wear a weight training belt for support if you are lifting heavy weights

◆ You may find it beneficial to train specific groups of muscles at each session – chest/shoulders one session, – legs/arms the next – back/abdominals the next for example – don't forget to warm up the whole body thoroughly

Seated Pull Downs

This machine works the shoulders and the back, and can be pulled down either in front of your body, or behind your neck. Your legs are fixed under a support to assist you in the movement which only works the area that you are pulling down on.

This machine works the same group of muscles which are worked when performing Shoulder Press see page 61.

Leg Extensions

This machine works the legs and will give you complete definition of your leg muscles. See exercise page 69.

Upright Rowing

This is the same exercise as performed with dumbbells (see page 56). The machine assists with the correct movement and is a very good exercise for beginners.

Incline Sit Ups

All fitness rooms will have an incline sit up bench, which will allow you to perform two exercises – the incline sit up and the hanging leg raises. You will have performed these exercises at home using free weights, during the earlier stages of your training and can continue them as part of your program.

Training for Competition

Bodybuilding requires hard work and determination to achieve objectives, even when constant training seems tough and fatigue grips your whole body.

Body building is a sport which requires strong commitment to hard work and strict dieting. But the physical achievements, pleasures of competition and the social aspects of the sport will bring their own unique rewards.

Before you decide to begin training for bodybuilding it is wise to discuss the demands of intense training with those already involved in the sport, and to make sure that you will have enough time to devote to your training program right from the start.

Dedication to Training

You must ensure that your lifestyle will be able to cope with the long hours of training and the inevitable fatigue associated with serious body building. Will you be able to accommodate your hours of weight training and cross training with your hours of work and your family life?

Before you begin to develop a personal training program, you must seek the advice and assistance of an experienced professional trainer who will help you to plan your diet and training schedule and organise your routines with specific competitions at the appropriate level, in mind. Your trainer will not only offer you valuable advice and assistance but will always be there to encourage you at times when your body is tired, your program seems hard and you might be tempted to find excuses not to train.

A beginner's body building program will involve working out at least three times per week – each session between one and two hours, concentrating on different muscle groups on different days, combined with aerobic cross training on the two days between weight training sessions.

Muscle mass is created when increasingly heavier weights are employed and fewer repetitions performed for each exercise. Although particular attention may be paid to specific areas of the body, such as chest and shoulders, for example, it is extremely important to train the whole body to allow the muscles to function in harmony.

Remember, muscles can only pull – they cannot push and therefore each group requires the assistance of strong opposing muscles to complete the movement successfully and safely. An evenly developed, well muscled body is far more attractive than an unevenly developed body and will be awarded more points in competition.

Laura's Story

Between the ages of 10 and 23, Laura competed successfully as a member of the British Judo Team and has been an aerobics instructor for fourteen years.

She began training with weights at The Riverside Gym which she runs with her husband Tony, who is also a bodybuilder.

With expertise and encouragement from her experienced trainer, Steve Waghorn, Laura entered two regional 'warm-up' competitions where she was placed fourth and second. Laura then came sixth of thirteen competitors in her first major qualifier competition, The Britain Finals, where she represented the South of England – after just six months of serious training. This now qualifies her to go on to represent Britain in the Universe Bodybuilding Championships.

Laura would emphasise that diet and nutrition play a very significant part in successful bodybuilding, and this must be controlled by a dietician or an expert who has the knowledge and experience to develop an effective personal diet to complement the vigorous training program.

Since her recent successes, Laura has appeared on local television and radio programs and in newspapers, prompting an enormous response from inspired women who wish to learn the secrets of her success.

But Laura would point out that her achievements would not have been possible without the expertise of a good coach, the full support of her husband, family and friends and true dedication and commitment to the hard work and strict dieting.

Andrew's Story

Andrew had been weight training for four years before he decided to begin competitive bodybuilding. Training hard with his first competition in mind, Andrew concentrated on creating muscle mass, bulking up to 15 stones (95.25kg) before beginning a strict diet which lasted three months.

The diet, consisting mainly of chicken breast, salad, vegetables and rice, was not easy to follow, particularly as specific measures of food have to be consumed every two-three hours – to maintain protein and carbohydrate levels – which was difficult while he was at work. At the end of his diet and training, he weighed 12 stones (76.20kg).

Andrew is the first to admit that training for competition was the hardest thing he had ever done, but with the help and invaluable support from his fiancée and Steve Waghorn, his trainer at The Riverside Gym, the result was that he was placed third in his first ever competition, and looks forward to the next.

Cross-Training

Swimming is excellent aerobic exercise and can be enjoyed by all the family.

As you begin to build up your fitness level you may wish to take up other sporting activities to vary your training and generally add interest to your program. This is often referred to as cross training. Your weight training program will increase your level of general fitness and help you to develop other sports skills, making your training more varied and interesting and enabling you to participate in a variety of activities where you may be enjoying exercise with a partner, an opponent, or with others in a group.

Most energetic sporting activities will be beneficial to your over-all training program, and those listed below are particularly useful for exercising specific muscle groups:

Running	**works upper body**
Aerobics	**works whole body**
Swimming	**works whole body – the water supports your weight and reduces stress on the muscles**
Badminton	**good all-round exercise**
Tennis	**good all-round exercise**
Cycling	**good exercise for arms, legs and back**

Forty minutes to an hour of cross training per week will help to improve your over-all fitness and should be incorporated into your personal fitness program. You will be able to choose an activity which will involve your partner, children or friends to ensure the exercises are both a social activity and beneficial to your training.

The following aerobic activities could easily be alternated to add interest and variety to your program.

Swimming

Swimming is an ideal exercise to begin your cross training. It is generally regarded as one of the best exercises for the whole body, working all the major muscle groups with the added benefit of the water supporting the weight of the body. By reducing the effect of gravity, the water reduces the stress that the exercise might otherwise cause.

Swimming is an activity which allows you to work at your own pace, choosing strokes which are most beneficial to your overall workout. It is important to build up the time and intensity of your swimming gradually.

Set yourself goals each session – to swim an increasing number of lengths of the pool, or continuously for a certain length of time. 'Aquafitness' is becoming a popular aerobic group exercise performed in water.

Exercising in water is something which can be enjoyed by people of all ages and fitness levels and is an ideal introduction to aerobic exercise for the beginner and excellent exercise for those recovering from athletic injuries, as it places minimal stress on all joints of the body.

The resistance of the water slows the movement of the exercise, impeding sharp or sudden movements which may cause muscle strains or ligament injuries. The water provides a weightless feeling which assists the body to perform movements which may be difficult or painful on land.

Skipping

Boxers skip to assist their all-round fitness, and many recent studies have shown that skipping for just five minutes each day can improve the health of the cardiovascular system.

Skipping is good all-round aerobic exercise and although many of us associate skipping with childhood playground memories, it is excellent exercise for adults too. Skipping is good for working the calves, buttocks, thighs, back and shoulders, and improves co-ordination.

A skipping rope is a very inexpensive addition to your fitness equipment, it can easily be taken with you when you are away from home, can be performed almost anywhere, and it is also fun!

Walking

Everyone can enjoy the pleasures and benefits of walking. Exercising at our own pace and perhaps in the company of others, walking can greatly improve overall fitness. Exercise taken in the fresh air in interesting surroundings will contribute to our general sense of health and well-being.

Walking can be easily introduced into your everyday routine – take the stairs instead of the elevator, walk to work or the shops instead of taking the car, walk the dog more often etc.

Once walking has become part of your daily routine, you can set yourself personal goals and plot a number of varied and interesting routes to build into your training program.

Choose routes which are 1 – 4 miles long (1.6 – 6.5km), depending on your fitness, and plan to walk your routes between two and four times every week.

TOP TIPS

◆ Begin slowly, and take time to build up the length of your walks

◆ Use your arms to assist you to walk fast, but choose a pace which you can maintain for the whole walk

◆ Breathe steadily and normally, do not over stress your body and cause breathlessness

◆ Keep your back straight and shoulders relaxed

◆ Wear loose, comfortable clothing

◆ Wear comfortable, sensible shoes designed for walking

◆ Keep to your timetable

◆ Don't forget to march on your rebounder when the weather prevents you from walking out of doors

It is not always necessary to walk or jog out of doors. The Quinton Treadmill, left, will allow you to exercise at the gym with the added advantage of being able to calculate your speed and distance travelled at the same time. Or jog at home using your rebounder (right) as part of your warm up and cross training.

Jogging

Jogging is a pace between walking and running and the speed will vary according to the individual. If you are jogging with a companion or two, it will be important to decide on a comfortable pace which suits you all and doesn't put unnecessary stress on the slower joggers.

To determine your ideal pace, you can do the talk test! This will help you to identify the fine line between jogging and running: If you were walking with a friend, you would be able to talk easily and in a relaxed manner. If you were then to run hard, your breathing would prevent you from speaking.

Jogging, however, should always be a relaxed and unhurried experience which still allows you to talk easily. If you find yourself unable to speak to your companion whilst jogging, you are going too fast. Happy jogging!

Cycling

Cycling is an excellent form of exercise which can be enjoyed by the whole family. Cycling works the leg muscles, and is very good for improving the cardiovascular system.

To begin with, you should look to cycle for at least 20 minutes each session. Remember to start off in a low gear and vary the route you take to add interest and reduce the risk of losing concentration on a too familiar route.

Be safety conscious and always wear protective head gear and suitable bright reflective clothing to allow other road users to see you clearly. Make sure your bicycle has reflective strips and adequate lights for cycling in bad weather or in the dark.

Include some hill work in your cycle training for beneficial effect, but don't be over-ambitious too early in your general training program.

Exercises to help improve your cycling include Dumbbell Press page 62, Sit Ups page 72, Hamstring Stretches page 38 and Upright Rowing page 56.

Inclement weather need not spoil your cycling. Most fitness clubs will have a number of exercise bicycles to enable you to concentrate on your workout without worrying about the traffic or the weather. The Bike by Cybex, right, features a computer aided distance and speed monitor.

The Tectrix VR Bike, above, combines the very latest in virtual reality technology with the comfort of a recumbent position designed to allow for increased muscle involvement.

This ingenious design even enables you to tip from side to side as you encounter corners on the route unfolding realistically on the screen before you. Pedal resistance and wind forces also increase and decrease appropriately in response to your actions and the terrain.

Saunas for relaxation

Saunas may also contribute to your fitness program and will promote relaxation and a general sense of well-being. Saunas are beneficial to the skin, deep cleansing through the loss of waste products from the pores, stimulating the circulation and allowing fresh blood supplies to reach the tissues quickly. The general warmth and feeling of well-being will help to relax both the muscles and the mind following a strenuous exercise session.

Contrary to popular belief, saunas are not a long term method of losing weight. Depending on the amount of time you spend in a sauna, you will lose a greater or lesser amount of weight, through water loss. This is then replaced immediately you drink liquid.

Saunas should not be taken less than one hour after food or by anyone who is medically unfit, or who has a history of cardiovascular problems or hypertension. Saunas should not be taken following intake of alcohol, or as a hang-over cure. Saunas dehydrate the body, and alcohol also dehydrates – the combination of the two could prove to be extremely dangerous.

If you have never taken a sauna before, it is wise to build up the time inside the sauna gradually, five minutes at a time, to acclimatise your body to the experience and make the most of the benefits. It is wise to remove any jewellery before entering a sauna, as it may become dangerously hot!

Always remember to take a drink of water, fruit juice or a soft drink after a sauna – do not drink alcohol. Do not step immediately into a cold shower following a sauna, as the shock may be too much – take a tepid shower first to allow your body to cool slightly.

Spending some time in a sauna (left) or a steam room (above), will cleanse the pores and relax both the mind and the muscles following a strenuous workout.

What could be better than a refreshing swim followed by a spa bath (below) after your demanding training session?
Pictures by courtesy of Tylo UK Limited.

Index of Exercises

Warm Up and Stretch

Ankle stretch:
Ankle roll — page 37
Back stretches:
General — page 39
Back (lower) stretch:
Wall stretches — page 38
Back (lower) & hip warm ups:
Straight overs
Hip swings – backwards and forwards
Swings – side to side — page 29
Buttock:
Stretch — page 39
Calf warm up:
Lifts — page 31
Chest & back warm ups:
Arms raise front
Arms raise back — page 27
Ham string:
Stretch — page 38
Hip warm up:
Side lunges — page 30
Neck & shoulder stretches:
Head rolls
Neck stretch
Shoulder Curls — page 32
Neck warm ups:
Turns
Nods — page 26
Rib stretches:
Forwards
Backwards — page 33
Thigh:
Stretch — page 37
Thigh (inner) & buttock stretches:
Butterflies
Cross-legged stretch — page 36
Torso stretches:
Side stretches
Seated side stretches — page 34
Torso & lower body stretches:
Torso stretches
Scissors
Front hip stretch — page 35
Torso warm ups:
Side bends
Torso circles — page 28

The Exercises

Abdomen:
Leg extensions — page 69
Crunch sit ups
Twisted sit ups — page 72
Reverse curls — page 73
Abdomen & waist:
Side bends — page 70
Back (lower), buttocks & thighs:
Dead lifts — page 52
Back (major):
Bent over rowing — page 54
Biceps:
Bicep curls
Kickbacks — page 65
Calf:
Standing calf raises — page 74
Chest:
Box press up — page 58
Press up — page 59
Hips, thighs & buttocks:
Forward lunges — page 43
Step ups — page 44
Legs & buttocks:
Side squats
French squats — page 42
Shoulders:
Flys — page 60
Dumbbell press — page 62
Shoulders (front):
Front shoulder lifts — page 64
Shoulders (inner & upper):
Upright rowing — page 56
Shoulders (outer):
Side lateral raise — page 63
Shoulders (top):
Shoulder press — page 61
Thighs (back):
Leg curl — page 50
Thighs (back) & buttocks:
Knee lift to rear — page 46
Thighs (inner & outer):
Raises — page 49
Triceps:
Overhead extension — page 66
Dips — page 68
Wrists:
Wrist curls — page 75

Acknowledgements

The author and publisher would like to express their sincere thanks to the following suppliers who very kindly allowed us to use photographs of their equipment, and for their helpful advice:

Forza Fitness Equipment Limited, Fourth Floor, Europe House, World Trade Centre, London E1 9AA, England, for photographs on front cover and pages 10, 21, 43, 45, 51, 55, 67, 85, 76, 90, 92 and 93.

Nautilus All in Fitness Limited, 43 Weir Road, Hemingford Grey, Huntingdon, Cambs, PE18 9EH, England for photographs on pages 48, 83 and 84.

Tylo UK Limited, Gratton Way, Roundswell Industrial Estate, Barnstaple EX1 3NL, England, for all photographs on pages 94 and 95.

Many thanks to our terrific models, Laura Church and Andrew Harland from **The Riverside Gym**, Wharf Road, Tovil, Maidstone, Kent, ME15 6RT, England and dance students Ceri Owen and Katie Costello.

We would also like to thank the manager and staff at **The Old Rectory Health & Fitness Club**, Farleigh Lane, Barming, Kent ME16 9LX, England, for their kind assistance and use of their excellent gym facilities and swimming pool featured on pages 80, 81, 82, 83 (top) and 88.